THE GOLDEN RING

Photographs by Vadim Gippenreiter
Text by Alexei Komech

CITIES OF OLD RUSSIA

Abbeville Press · Publishers
New York · London · Paris

Library of Congress Cataloging-in-Publication Data
Gippenreĭter, Vadim Evgen'evich.
    The golden ring: cities of old Russia/photographs of old Russia/
    photographs by Vadim Gippenreiter; text by Alexei Komech.
    p.   cm.
    Translated from the Russian.
    ISBN 1–55859–216–4
    1. Architecture — Russian S.F.S.R.   2. Church architecture —
    Russian S.F.S.R.   3. City planning — Russian S.F.S.R. —
    History.   4. Russian S.F.S.R. — History.
    I. Komech, A.I. (Aleksei I.) II. Title
    NA1181. G56 1991
    720'.947 — dc20   91–10687
                                                      CIP

First edition

This book was designed and produced by
Laurence King Ltd, London
Translated by Robin and Julia Whitby
Designed by Mikhail Anikst

Frontispiece
The Cathedral of the Dormition,
Rostov (mid- to late seventeenth
century).

Title spread
The Holy Saviour-Yakovlevsky
Monastery in Rostov, seen from
Lake Nero.

Front jacket
View of the Trinity-St Sergius
Monastery from beyond the kremlin
wall, Zagorsk.

Back jacket
Interior of the Church of the
Resurrection, Rostov.

Back flap
Top: A sixteenth-century icon
depicting St Nicholas surrounded
by scenes from his life, Pskov.
Bottom: A sixteenth-century icon,
'The Descent into Hell', Pskov.

CONTENTS

INTRODUCTION

Medieval cities have a particular fascination and – paradoxically – relevance for modern man. The atmosphere they evoke can put us in touch with neglected or discarded artistic, spiritual and moral values, and so contribute to the process of regeneration taking place in contemporary life. We are rightly proud of the dynamism of our modern age and the rapid pace of its scientific and material development; we retain confidence in the idea of progress and our mastery of nature. In our relationship with the past, however, we seem to have lost as much as we have gained. In particular, attention to life's spiritual and religious dimensions, and the development of moral qualities and artistic vision have been greatly devalued in our time. Culture and art no longer enjoy the intense respect paid to them by society until the nineteenth century.

An ancient city, with its exotic beauty and splendid monuments, attracts us initially as a tangible proof of the history of a society; but it should also become an inseparable part of our contemporary culture, contributing breadth and depth to the education of our children, enrichment to our work as adults and enjoyment to our declining years. In visiting such cities we may find release from the tensions of everyday life as we allow ourselves to sense the flow of centuries, even millennia, to muse on the fate of individuals and societies, and to admire humans' genius and inspiration.

An individual city will reflect the true character of its past inhabitants. Ancient Russian cities differ from their Western counterparts in a number of ways. Perhaps the most striking difference is that they are not very 'urban' in our modern sense of the word; not an ensemble of houses and joined façades forming streets and neighbourhoods, but rather a much less dense collection of separate properties with houses set in their own land. To be sure, some large medieval cities – such as Novgorod, Pskov and Moscow – did develop a kind of urban density, with streets forming uninterrupted corridors consisting of wood-laid pavements and fencing relieved only by gates; but such fencing was never higher than about eight feet, and the wooden (or, until the seventeenth century, very occasional stone) buildings were disposed behind them at various angles to the road and gave the city as a whole a sense of flexible composition and a free use of space. Buildings were often separated from each other by waste land, orchards or vegetable gardens. In the late medieval period some areas of a town were given a distinctive character with steep and sometimes elaborately patterned roofs.

Another distinguishing feature of old Russian cities is the great abundance of churches. Fifteenth-century Novgorod contained about one hundred and fifty (including the surrounding monasteries); Moscow boasted even more; and even eighteenth-century Suzdal, which comprised some four hundred households, possessed nearly fifty churches. This is very different from a typical Western European town of that size, which might have only one or two large churches. The Russian city landscape was made up of a number of small churches nestling among larger ones (called *sobors* in Russian and normally translated as 'cathedrals', although they are not cathedrals in the Western European sense: the seat of a bishop). All of these silhouettes, including domes and bell towers, created a powerful visual metaphor, expressing, through the shapes and materials of the physical world, the splendour of the spiritual realm. Such cities were defined by their churches, and also by the lovely palaces and mansions of the nobility, and by the walls and towers of the fortifications – somewhat as our modern cities are characterized mainly by their banks, hotels, offices and shopping centres.

A third feature of Russian cities was the absence of a clear-cut boundary, for they were usually surrounded by monastic and other settlements. In the course of time the growing city might absorb such outlying areas, only for more monasteries and hamlets to spring up outside it. The remarkable monasteries on the southern edge of Moscow were founded and ex-

Left

Rostov. View looking up at the southwest tower of the kremlin wall.

Above right

Zagorsk. View from the west. The domes of the Cathedral of the Dormition can be seen behind the walls in the centre of the picture, with the eighteenth-century bell tower on their right.

7

The Trinity-St Sergius Lavra, Zagorsk

The Church of the Nativity of Christ, Yaroslavl

The Dmitrievsky Cathedral, Vladimir

The Church of the Epiphany at Zapskovye, Pskov

The Cathedral of St Sophia, Kiev

The Rostov Kremlin

BALTIC SEA

Lake Onega

Lake Ladoga

Lake Chudskoe

Novgorod

Lake Ilmen

Izborsk

Pskov

Pechori

Volkhov

Kostroma

Yaroslavl

Pereslavl

Suzdal

Rostov

Vladimir

Bogolyubovo

Zagorsk

Moscow

Neman

Kiev

Dnieper

Don

Volga

BLACK SEA

AZOV SEA

CASPIAN SEA

Map showing the distribution of medieval Russian cities. Kiev and Novgorod were the principal cities of eleventh and twelfth century Rus. Gradually Slavs colonized the northeastern territories in which the Vladimir-Suzdal principality was to flourish in the course of the twelfth century. After the Tatar invasions and the consequent mass impoverishment of the populations in the south of Rus, it fell to Novgorod and Pskov to preserve the continuity and richness of medieval Russian life. Moscow gradually established itself as the political centre of Rus, becoming a Grand Ducal city in the fourteenth century. The southern trade route lost its former significance as the route northward, to the Volga (and, from the sixteenth century, further – to Vologda and, via Archangel, on to Western Europe) gained in importance. It was on this northern route that the Trinity-St Sergius Monastery (later Zagorsk), Pereslavl, Rostov and Yaroslavl developed into major centres of population, trade and art. In the seventeenth century the growth of trade along the Volga stimulated the rise of many splendid cities, including Kostroma.

panded in this way; and the landscape around Novgorod and Pskov owed – and to some extent still owes – much of its charm to a similar process.

Another important element in such cities was the presence of beautiful natural landscape even at their very centres, usually in the form of one or more broad rivers, flanked by uncluttered embankments. A natural pace of life, within an environment created on a human scale with pleasing asymmetry, always triumphed over the imposition of regularity and regimentation in Russian cities.

A thousand years ago the Varangians, a Scandinavian people, knew ancient Rus by the name 'Gardarika', which meant the land of cities. Many ninth- and tenth-century Slavic settlements were protected by earthen ramparts and walls constructed of wood or rough stones. Indeed, the Russian word for town, *gorod*, was originally the word for fortifications.

Usually these fortified settlements extended along high river banks on promontories or at the confluences of rivers. Rivers provided both transport and defence, offering a city protection on one, two or even three of its flanks. In the course of time, as the population increased and building spilled beyond the fortified area, a trading quarter, or *posad*, would form on the outskirts of the town. Soon the *posad* acquired its own fortification, while the original nucleus of the settlement became the citadel, or kremlin, of the enlarged city.

This general pattern of development varied greatly according to geographical, economic and political conditions. A city might evolve from a single settlement, or from the merging of several settlements, together with the construction of a fortress between them. Many were founded by princes; others grew gradually from trading posts favourably situated at the crossroads between other cities. Some flourished immediately; a few had to wait hundreds of years for their moment of glory.

There are approximately two hundred Russian cities that may be termed 'historic', in that their way of life, their appearance and their culture reflect the country's past. This book is concerned with nine of the oldest and most lavishly endowed with architectural monuments.

The title 'Mother of Russian Cities' rightfully belongs to Kiev. There are traces of a fifth-century settlement to be found in the area, but the true origins of the city really date from the eighth and ninth centuries, when it became, by virtue of its favourable location, the administrative centre of the eastern Slav territories. It became a principality and subsequently the capital of a grand duchy and a mighty state.

Kiev is situated on the high right bank of the River Dnieper. Nowadays we tend to think that a city on a river should boast splendid embankments with fine buildings – in other words that it should 'face' the river – but medieval Russian cities lined their rivers with fortifications or commonplace buildings of various kinds, such as docks and warehouses. The upper part of Kiev formed the enclosed central nucleus, which was complemented by the lower town – a trading quarter occupying a narrow, low strip on the right bank beneath the hills, where business was done and boats went back and forth.

Introduction

The adoption of Christianity by Kiev's ruler, Grand Duke Vladimir I (980–1015), in 988 transformed the appearance of Kievan cities, whose centres were henceforward to be dominated by churches and great cathedrals. The first of these was the Church of the Tithe (completed 996), which was built on the orders of Vladimir and which towered over the surrounding royal palaces.

The Christianization of Kiev also heralded fundamental changes in the mentality of Slav society, which was now obliged to turn from its pagan culture and address an already ancient world civilization. A new architecture, influenced by that of Byzantium, remains perhaps the most visible embodiment of the remarkable blossoming of art that occurred in eleventh-century Rus. Following the example of Constantinople, the principal Russian cities – notably Kiev and Novgorod – constructed magnificent cathedrals dedicated to Sophia, or the Holy Wisdom. Like their namesake in Constantinople, they dominate the skylines of their respective cities. Sophia of Kiev (c.1050) remains, in spite of the houses built around it in the nineteenth and twentieth centuries, the spiritual, artistic and architectural centre of the city.

The cathedral was conceived on the most grandiose scale of any Byzantine church of its time. It had five naves (two more were added in the seventeenth century) with two-storey galleries running around the interior and two single-storey galleries flanking the exterior walls, with stair towers built into the galleries on the western side. The cathedral is crowned by thirteen cupolas, whose subtle rhythms create a splendid pyramidal composition.

The interior is remarkable for the perfection of its architectural forms and the fortunate preservation of its mosaics and frescoes. We can still be moved by the thought that this self-contained cosmos, populated by figures from the Bible and from holy legends, has attracted worshippers for nearly a thousand years.

From the central crossing of the cathedral, one can look up into the main cupola, where a mosaic represents Christ Pantocrator surrounded by angels. In the central apse, the Virgin is depicted as defender of the human race and of the new city chosen by God: Kiev itself. Columns on the east side are carved with the figures of the Archangel Gabriel and the Virgin Mary, seemingly acting out the Annunciation in three-dimensional space. A marvellous rhythm unites the figures, each of which is imbued with a sense of spirituality, discipline and harmony.

The interior as a whole wonderfully evokes the spirit of the Christian ceremonial art of eleventh-century Rus. The special position of the grand duke himself is symbolized by a spacious choir stall built specifically for his use. In deliberate contrast with the dark vaulted sections under the choirs, the central crossing gives a striking impression of light and air. The south transept contains a portrayal of the family of Sophia's creator, Yaroslav the Wise (1019–54), presenting Christ with the cathedral he has constructed.

Yaroslav situated the cathedral at the centre of a city that he had first significantly increased in size and then surrounded by an earth rampart strengthened with wooden walls and stone gates. (The remains of the principal, Golden Gate have been preserved.) In the course of the eleventh and twelfth centuries many monastries and churches were to adorn Kiev. In addition, a royal residence was built at Vyshgorod, six miles away; and, somewhat nearer to the city, a group of monasteries grew up, the most important of which was the Kievo-Pecherksy Monastery.

In the twelfth century Kievan Rus split into three principalities which, in spite of the dynastic ties binding their rulers, were frequently at war with each other. For three centuries, in fact, Rus was transformed into dozens of increasingly tiny principalities. Many of these preserved a highly individual character. Nevertheless, Kiev itself remained the model of a capital city until the advent of the Mongols in 1240.

Interior of St Sophia's Cathedral in Kiev (mid-eleventh century). This general view of the cathedral is extraordinarily impressive, including in a single sweep its principal works of art: mosaics depicting Christ Pantocrator, the Apostles and the Evangelists in the cupola, and the Heavenly Liturgy and the Annunciation on the east columns in the apse. At its centre, at the rear of the apse, is the huge figure of the Virgin Orans, executed in mosaic and symbolizing the divine protection both of the newly Christianized population of Rus and the new city chosen by God – Kiev itself.

Introduction

Christ Pantocrator and Archangels, mosaic in the cupola of St Sophia's Cathedral, Kiev. Partly restored in the late nineteenth century by Mikhail Vrubel.

Second only to Kiev was the city of Novgorod. Although destined for subjugation in later centuries, it has retained to this day the imprint of its original glory to a greater degree than almost any other medieval Russian city. Early eleventh-century monumental churches, with the church of Sophia in their midst, created a city centre of imposing dimensions, in which traces of grand ducal might and power mingle with later evidence of the Novgorodian tradition of 'freemen', the unique system of government based on the *veche*, or popular assembly, which flourished between the twelfth and the fifteenth centuries. The early princely style was replaced by a simpler, more sober and dramatic approach in the late twelfth century—an era of war and invasion—which became lighter and more festive in the fifteenth century.

Along with churches, the most important type of building in medieval Russia was fortifications. The fortifications of Russian cities in the pre-Mongol period were constructed of wood and earth; recently some stonework has also been found (at Izborsk and possibly Ladoga), but this is dry-stone walling of no very durable construction. Such fortifications could never provide decisive protection, and battles were lost and won on open ground. The absence of major stone fortifications was a root cause of the rapid and shattering defeats at the hands of the Mongols in the thirteenth century.

In the fourteenth century, intensive construction of stone fortifications was begun in Novgorod, Moscow and other cities. The inhabitants of Pskov were particularly zealous in the defence of their city. Situated on the western marches of Russian territory, Pskov was especially vulnerable to incursions and continually involved in clashes with Lithuanian warrior tribes and the Teutonic Order of Knights. By the sixteenth century five lines of stone walling had been erected on the city's open, hitherto undefended flank; they were to prove their worth on several occasions.

Until the fourteenth century Pskov grew in the shadow of Novgorod, under whose administrative authority it came. As we might expect, there was a general similarity between the two cities, especially in their social and political arrangements (including the *veche*), and Pskov was strongly influenced by the Novgorodian artistic tradition. From the fourteenth century onwards, however, when Pskov achieved independence, the city rapidly developed an aesthetic style of its own.

Compared with that of Novgorod, Pskovian masonry architecture seems less inclined to the epic. The emotional appeal of Pskovian art is more immediate, and, in the case of icons, frequently more disturbing. The designs of its churches contain more separate elements and impart a greater sense of mobility. The picturesque is prized above the monumental. A moving sense of faith imbues the interiors of Pskov churches, whose atmosphere is one of intense piety.

Vladimir is completely different in character. Its sumptuous royal art is distinguished by nobility of form, together with a sense of confidence, energy and creative will. White stone churches rise as in some magical vision from the high bank over the River Klyazma, where Prince Vladimir Monomakh (1113–25) pursued his ambition to build a city in the image of Kiev.

Vladimir's unique place among Russian cities is due largely to the splendour of the Cathedral of the Dormition of the Virgin, in which until 1432, the Russian prince chosen to succeed to the grand duchy was crowned. A special glory of the cathedral is the series of murals by Andrei Rublev (1408); they are, in fact, the only works of this great master to be identified and authenticated by contemporary chronicles. The cathedral was to serve as the model for the Cathedral of the Dormition in Moscow, completed in 1479; indeed, its five-domed structure became the canonical norm for many sixteenth- and seventeenth-century churches.

A royal residence, Bogolyubovo, was built on the outskirts of Vladimir. Nearby, on the flood-meadows at the confluence of the Nerl and the Klyazma, rose the exceptionally fine Church of the Intercession, as moving and lyrical in its way as the school of painting associated with Vladimir. Whereas the principal churches of Kiev, Novgorod and Pskov were dedicated to Sophia and to the Holy Trinity, the rulers of Vladimir entrusted their city and territory to the protection of the Blessed Virgin. This is reflected in the dedication of the city's most important church to the Dormition and also in the fact that Vladimir was the birthplace of the Feast of the Intercession of the Virgin.

The Tatar invasion of the thirteenth century, with the devastation this entailed, and the subordination of Russian principalities to the Tatar empire of the Golden Horde had, inevitably, a deleterious effect upon Russian art. However, painting and architecture began to revive and to develop in new ways after the first decisive defeat of the Tatars at the Battle of Kulikovo Pole in 1380. By the fifteenth century, when the Tatars were on the defensive, Russian art was flourishing once more.

The Trinity-St Sergius *Lavra*, or Monastery (now the town of Zagorsk), located some fifty miles north of Moscow, is an outstanding example of this rebirth. The monastery was founded by the extraordinary Russian hero and zealot Sergius Radonezhsky (1322–92). Great white stone churches dating from the fifteenth century became the foundation of the monastery, whose construction was to continue for another three hundred years, during which time a sensitive collaboration between architects and artists transformed it into one of the most revered places in Russia.

Monasteries were crucial to the development of Russian culture and of Russian cities in the fifteenth and sixteenth centuries. They were pillars of spirituality and great educational centres and, equally, the source of generous and richly-endowed commissions. Splendid sixteenth-century monastery ensembles transformed the appearance of many Russian cities. Often they were the work of architects who were also responsible for the construction of the capital of Muscovy, Moscow, and they brought to the buildings of these far-flung areas a similar monumentalism and grandeur of scale, frequently creating the model on which a local tradition was founded. Such was the case in Zagorsk, Pereslavl, Yaroslavl and Suzdal.

The role of the Suzdal monasteries is exceptionally significant. Suzdal is a small city which has now lost the importance it had in the twelfth and thirteenth centuries. By the fifteenth century, when it was effectively absorbed by the Moscow state, it no longer disposed of the wealth required to restore its magnificent, but half-collapsed white stone thirteenth-century cathedral. Suzdal's northern marches were graced by two monumental churches, the Intercession and the Holy Saviour of Yefim, together with the Rizpolozhensky convent; in addition, the Cathedral of the Nativity of the Virgin and the nearby episcopal palaces were rebuilt. The development of the *posad* (trading quarter) in the seventeenth and eighteenth centuries, including its many churches, integrated city and monasteries into a unified whole, but the sixteenth-century buildings remain the most splendid elements in the city panorama.

In Pereslavl the sixteenth-century monasteries were situated close to the city but never merged with it. However, their presence in the city landscape, together with a masterpiece of twelfth-century architecture, the Cathedral of the Transfiguration of the Saviour, alters our perception of the intimate eighteenth- and nineteenth-century buildings which make up the town, saving them from mere provincialism.

From the sixteenth century onwards, the development of Russian cities proceeded within the unified state, governed from Moscow, and on the basis of a generally accepted architectural style. However, this did not exclude great variety in the appearance and way of life of individual cities. The importance of the Volga trade route increased dramatically at the end of the sixteenth century, when the founding of Archangel on the White Sea made sea trade with Western Europe possible. Four of the cities in this book – Zagorsk, Pereslavl, Rostov and Yaroslavl – were situated on this route and owed much of their prosperity to this development.

The prosperity of the Volga cities in the seventeenth century allots them a unique position in Russian culture. These were no mere satellites of Moscow but thoroughly independent artistic centres of major importance. The growth in their power and influence, which had begun in the sixteenth century, was increased by the events known as the Time of Troubles, in the early seventeenth century, when they became the bastion of the struggle to expel the Polish invaders and to liberate Moscow.

The wealth, business acumen and craftsmanship abounding among the people of Yaroslavl produced the great monumental churches which were erected on estates and elsewhere in the city. These were larger in scale than the modest parish churches of late seventeenth-century Moscow; their inspiration, rather, was sixteenth-century Yaroslavl itself, and in particular the Holy Monastery of the Transfiguration of Our Saviour. The city skyline, together with its view over the Kotorislya valley, was dominated by great five-domed churches, their exteriors marvellously decorated and their interiors adorned with vast frescoes and murals and sumptuous iconostases.

Russian city skylines were dominated not only by onion-domes but increasingly, in the sixteenth and seventeenth centuries, by the high tent, or hipped, roofs with which churches and bell towers were crowned. Suzdal contains some especially fine examples of this style.

So intensive was the blossoming of the Volga artistic tradition that it influenced the appearance of even the most ancient cities. A quite spectacular work of this period, the Rostov kremlin, resembles the central ensemble of early Russian cities but was the product of a single and unified concept. It governs Rostov to such an extent that tourists often mistakenly identify the city with the kremlin alone.

The great seventeenth-century cathedrals continued to dominate the Volga cities even after the construction of new and splendid city centres in the eighteenth and nineteenth centuries. Kostroma is a most attractive example of Russian classicism, but its true historical significance and scale is determined by the Ipatiev Monastery and the Church of the Resurrection on the Debra. Following the barbaric destruction of the central Cathedral of the Dormition and the churches of the Old City in the 1930s, it fell to these two remaining masterpieces to provide a focus for the panorama which embraces both river and city.

The splendour of each of the above-mentioned cities had its echoes in many neighbouring towns, monasteries and villages; but it is in those few cities selected for this book that we can best grasp the essence of Russia, her history and her culture. The reader may experience something of the atmosphere of these cities thanks to the superb artistry of the photographer, Vadim Gippenreiter. The finest photographer of nature in the Soviet Union, a passionate lover of the Russian countryside and Russian culture, Gippenreiter is totally dedicated to expressing their beauty in his art. He has captured some of the most wonderful moments in the life of these medieval cities and monuments – moments when their unique charm is particularly evident. The weather, the time of day, the seasons of the year, special effects of the light – he has selected all these elements with endless patience. The translucent quality of his photography, whether bursting with light and energy or pensive and tender, is the perfect medium in which to convey the beauty of old Russia, a medium that can be surpassed only by the reality of the subject itself.

Suzdal, tent roof on the Dormition Refectory Church of the Saviour-Yakovlevsky Monastery (c. 1525). Between the sixteenth and the eighteenth centuries similar tent roofs, some functional, others purely decorative and elegant, frequently replaced the traditional onion domes on churches and bell towers, becoming an inseparable element of urban and monastic skylines. The tent roof of the Church of the Dormition, one of the earliest in Rus, is part of the superb tent-roof ensemble which crowns the Suzdal kremlin as well as the Holy Saviour of St Yefim and Pokrovsky monasteries.

Introduction

16

NOVGOROD

The name Novgorod, or 'new town', may seem a rather surprising one for one of the most ancient Russian cities. It refers to the birth of a city in the tenth century but also implies the existence of an even older city, hitherto unknown to us.

Novgorod is situated on the River Volkhov, by Lake Ilmen. The river flows from this lake northwards into Lake Ladoga, from which a further waterway leads on to the Baltic Sea. Novgorod owes its prosperity to this route, well known in ancient times, which was the beginning of a much longer one stretching, as the saying went, 'from the Vikings to the Greeks'. Scholars used to identify the older city with Ladoga (situated near the lake), an important settlement as early as the eighth and ninth centuries, but two new theories have recently challenged this suggestion. One places the old settlement at Gorodishche, a village one and one-quarter miles from Novgorod, on a hill by the source of the Volkhov. The other posits three ancient settlements on the site of the present Novgorod, eventually merging to form a fortified centre surrounded by a fence; this merged entity became known as Novgorod. The original villages were populated by various ethnic groups, which probably explains why the region was

Above
Twelfth-century enamel miniature used in the gold setting of a nineteenth-century *oklad*, or icon cover, in Novgorod Museum.

Left
Icon, 'The Worship of St Peter's Fetters' (detail), from the Church of St Peter and St Paul in Kozhevniki.

originally divided into three areas known as 'the Slav End', 'the Prussian End' and 'the Merevsky End' (the latter occupied by an ancient people called the Merya).

The most important elements of Novgorod's social system were the powerful landowners, or boyars. They made up its ruling council, an electoral college or *posadnichestvo*, and dominated the all-city gatherings known as *veche*. In ninth-century Rus it was common for powerful princes (with their armies) to be invited by a town's citizens to assume responsibility for the defence and administration of a region. Such rulers gradually increased their authority and eventually constituted the political foundations for the flowering of a huge state – Kievan Rus. This hegemony included Novgorod, which became not only the second city after Kiev itself but a kind of joint kingdom, for the eldest son of the prince of Kiev usually ruled over the city before succeeding to his father's throne. The power of the boyars and *posadnik* (governor) was unquestionably subordinate to the authority of the prince.

The basic elements of Novgorod's architectural ensemble were laid down in the early twelfth century. During the Second World War many of its buildings were severely damaged or destroyed, but they have been faithfully restored and reconstructed. Medieval Novgorod spread from both banks of the river – the western side developing into the citadel, called the Sophia Side; the eastern into the Market Side. The river itself is the principal feature of a composition combining, in one great sweep, the urban ensemble with the breadth and openness of the low, flat countryside. The epic scale of the vista still evokes the respect in which the city was once held.

The city consisted mainly of the large properties of the boyars – approximately 165 by 230 feet – whose borders were fixed towards the end of the twelfth century and remained unchanged until the sixteenth. These domains were surrounded by palisades made of vertical sharpened poles with gates opening onto the streets. The streets, between 9 and 20 feet wide, were paved with wood and led directly down to the river; originally development was confined to these streets, but by the fourteenth century buildings were springing up everywhere, between the streets as well as along them.

Icon, 'The Battle of the Novgorodians and the Suzdalians, or the Miracle of the Holy Sign', from the eighteenth-century Church of Nicholas of Katchanov. This icon commemorates the events of 1169, when Suzdalian forces besieging Novgorod were decisively repelled by the Novgorodians, who ascribed their victory to the icon of Our Lady of the Holy Sign, a work particularly revered in Novgorod. The bird's-eye view of Novgorod depicts the St Sophia and Torgovaya areas surrounded by ramparts and walls. In the foreground, behind the wall near the tower, we see the Novgorodians, bearing their icon.

Novgorod

View of the kremlin from the Torgovaya Side. The ancient walls and towers were replaced by new fortifications in the late sixteenth and early seventeenth centuries. Behind these are the high tower of the archbishop's palace and the bell tower.

Beyond is St Sophia's Cathedral, which became the central element of the urban panorama from the eleventh century.

View south, on the Lake Ilmen side, looking from the Kokui tower of the kremlin. The broad, open view with, along the skyline, the Resurrection and Annunciation Monasteries and, to the left, the Churches of the Annunciation at Gorodishche and of Our Saviour, is an enduring symbol of the national heritage. The buildings date principally from the twelfth to the fifteenth centuries.

Novgorod

The Novgorodians preparing to repel the onslaught of the army of Vladimir-Suzdal in 1169. Above the warriors, streaming in the wind, are their flags and banners, which are painted and embroidered with symbols of the crucifixion. Detail from the icon 'The Miracle of the Holy Sign', mid-fifteenth century. (See page 20.)

The streets were linked by narrow lanes and wider roads running parallel to the contours of the river banks. This attractive picture was completed by the little River Fedorov meandering through the market quarter. In the twelfth century the city was surrounded by an earthen wall fortified with wood, part of which survives today.

The Christianization of Rus in the late tenth century ensured that Novgorod's architecture would be dominated by churches. Until the mid-twelfth century only a few were built, but their majestic dimensions determined the vast scale of the urban panorama. The influence of the thousand-year traditions of classical and Byzantine architecture, which spread to Novgorod from Kiev, explains the high artistic standard of the very earliest buildings. The Cathedral of St Sophia (1045-52), in the centre of the citadel, was commissioned by Grand Duke Vladimir.

In many respects the Novgorod Cathedral of St Sophia resembles its namesake in Kiev, built by Vladimir's father, Yaroslav the Wise. Its five onion domes, external gallery (now removed) and stepped tower are typical of several cathedrals built in the mid-eleventh century. It vividly reflects the royal culture of the time and its aspirations to a ceremonial, powerful and formal style. Many of the special features of Novgorodian style are already apparent – the monumental dimensions, especially the height, and the dominance of powerful, epic forms over lyrical, gentle motifs.

St Sophia was built at a time when princely authority was at its height, but by the beginning of the twelfth century the political balance of power was already in the process of change. The boyar nobility yearned for the absolute power they had enjoyed in earlier times; and the archbishop was playing an increasingly influential role. It was he, for example, who commissioned the frescoes for the cathedral in 1108, although the building work, done by the *artel* (a cooperative team of artisans) remained under the authority of the prince. Succession to the throne of Kiev by the ruler of Novgorod had been strictly observed since the tenth century; the city was therefore richly adorned with buildings symbolizing the authority of princely power, which in reality was on the wane.

In the eleventh century a royal residence was built near the market and opposite the citadel. It is associated with the name of Yaroslav and known as the Great Yaroslav Court. In 1113 the Cathedral of St Nicholas was constructed adjacent to it. Together with St Sophia, this five-domed Byzantine building forms the focus of the city's central ensemble. An identical church, the Annunciation, was built at nearby Gorodishche, where the earlier settlement was revived and a similar residence established.

Between 1119 and 1130 an imposing cathedral, dedicated to St George, was rebuilt in the Yuriev (George) Monastery on the left bank of the Volkhov opposite Gorodishche. The two churches together created a kind of gateway leading from Lake Ilmen, uniting the sweep of the natural landscape with the buildings of Novgorod, two miles north.

On the northern edge of the city, on the right bank of the Volkhov, yet another cathedral was erected, that of the Nativity of the Virgin (1117-19) belonging to the St Anthony Monastery.

In 1136 the citizens of Novgorod arrested and subsequently expelled Prince Vsevolod and his family. Henceforward ultimate power resided with the boyars and their elected *posadnik*. The prince now became a subordinate figure whose powers – mainly as a military leader – were strictly limited by constitutional agreement. (The Novgorodians' irreverent attitude towards their prince was tersely expressed in the saying 'If the prince is no good, into the mud with him.') The authority of the bishop (now the archbishop) increased significantly; among his other prerogatives, he was now in charge of the *artel*.

Numerous wooden and a few masonry churches were now built in Novgorod along the wide thoroughfares running parallel to the river. Increasingly they were commissioned by families or groups of merchants, or by local residents, and were correspondingly more modest than those built by the princes, lacking stair towers and spacious choirs. Two examples are the Church of the Annunciation at Myachino (1179) and the Church of St Peter and St Paul (1192) on Sinichya Hill.

Even royal commissions now had a simpler aspect. An example is the Church of Our Saviour (1198) on Nereditsa Hill, near Gorodishche, the last church to be commissioned by a Novgorod prince. It is a small, single-domed building with façades crowned by *zakomary*.

Building technology was in the process of change. Churches of the princely era were a mixture of stone and brick, similar to those of Kiev. Now stone predominated, with brick being used only for vaults and inset pilasters. Stucco and painted façades gave way to simple whitewashed walls whose uneven surfaces gave their buildings a primitive appearance. Art in general was becoming simpler and forms more disciplined. Nevertheless, the overall rhythm of gently rounded movement typical of Byzantine interiors (clearly reflected in the exteriors of twelfth-century Russian churches) saved this style from decline into the primitive and archaic. A certain *gravitas* imparts an epic and universal quality to these buildings.

The interiors of Novgorod churches now lost the sense of structured spaciousness that had distinguished their early twelfth-century predecessors; choirs were reduced to semi-enclosed chambers and chapels were reached by steps set into the walls.

In the early thirteenth century the architecture of Novgorod was unexpectedly stimulated by the arrival of craftsmen from Smolensk, commissioned by the merchant community to build the Church of Paraskeva Pyatnitsa (1207) in the market centre next to the Yaroslav Court. This impressive church, dedicated to the patron saint of commerce and housekeeping, combines a solid presence with a strong sense of movement, expressed in its trefoil-gabled roof, round-arched covered porches and clusters of attached columns.

Another outstanding church of the early 1200s is the small Church of the Nativity of the Virgin. The lines of its graceful trefoil gables are edged by parallel recessing on the façades.

The subsequent development of Novgorod was sharply restricted by the calamity that afflicted the whole of medieval Russia, namely the Mongol invasion. Although Novgorod escaped actual war damage, it was forced to pay exorbitant tribute to the Golden Horde. Construction virtually ceased for fifty years and revived only at the very end of the thirteenth century. The major figure in this renewed activity was the archbishop, who commanded two building *artels*. A considerable number of churches was built – most of them in the citadel itself or in the outlying areas. This period saw the completion of a ring of approximately twenty monasteries at a radius of between two-thirds of a mile and two miles from the city, creating an ensemble of striking complexity, richness and spirituality.

Churches dating from the first half of the fourteenth century are not impressive in size (about 30 to 40 feet high). Whereas twelfth-century buildings had rather large windows, those in buildings dating from the fourteenth are little more than narrow slits. The generally dark interiors are illuminated by sudden shafts of light, which create an atmosphere of drama.

Novgorodian architecture continued to flourish all through the second half of the fourteenth and into the fifteenth century. Most construction took place in the city, for the republic of the boyars was in its heyday, and it was they – together with other rich citizens – who were in a position to commission new buildings. Within a hundred years the overall shape of Novgorod was defined by the completion of stone walls around the kremlin and the rest of the town.

Architecture was, more than ever, considered an important part of civic life. Churches in the process of construction vied with one another in their complexity of design and the decorative elegance of their façades. The consecration of a new church was marked by a celebration, led by the archbishop and the choir of St Sophia's, in which the whole city was involved.

Churches increased in size (up to about 50 by 55 feet) and became generally more imposing. Façades were articulated by wide pilasters leading up to high trefoil gables. The finest of them are the churches of St Theodore Stratilates (1360-61) and, especially, Our Saviour of the Transfiguration on Elijah Street (1374). Its massive dimensions are organized with particular power and grace. Two-tiered pilasters create a kind of bas-relief frame crowned by trefoil gables. There are two rows of windows and niches which form elaborate and beautiful pyramidal designs in the central areas. The walls are decorated with crosses – some in relief, others incised. The apse has a two-tiered arcade in bas-relief similar to that of certain European Romanesque churches.

Novgorod's churches are memorable for their monumental and epic quality, which particularly strikes the visitor approaching from a distance. Perhaps even more remarkable are the interiors, whose gloomy grandeur is inseparable from the paintings that adorn them. The most interesting example of this relationship is the Church of Our Saviour of the Transfiguration, in which the frescoes of Theophanes the Greek, dating from 1378, have survived.

The Cathedral of St Sophia,
Novgorod (1045–52). View over
the domes from the west.

Novgorod

Kratir, or liturgical vessel for wine, made from silver gilt, embossed and engraved. Dating from the first half of the twelfth century, this is an excellent example of Novgorodian work. On the rim is an inscription in medieval Russian: *piitye ot neya vsi, se yest krov moya novovo zaveta* ('drink all ye, this be the blood of my new testament'). Around the base are inscribed the names of Petril and his wife Varvara who commissioned the piece; and underneath, the signature of the artist: 'Lord, help thy servant Florovi, Bratilo, who made this.'

Novgorod

Image of the Saviour, detail from
kratir.

Christ holding the spirit of the
Virgin in his hands, detail from
the icon 'The Dormition of the
Virgin' (late fifteenth century),
from the village of Kuritskoye.
The gravity of the image and the
tension and drama with which it
is imbued are typical of
Novgorodian art of this period.

The Church of Our Saviour of the Transfiguration on Elijah Street (1374). Commissioned by the Boyar Vasily Danilovich and others who lived in the street, this is the finest, most grandiose and most highly decorated example of fourteenth-century Novgorodian architecture. The windows are arranged in a pyramidal design. The façades are ornamented with crosses, in intaglio on the lower walls, and in high relief on the upper.

Novgorod

The Church of St Theodore Stratilates (1361). The church was built by the *posadnik*, or governor, of Novgorod, Semen Andreyevich; the *trapeznaya* (refectory) and bell tower were added in the seventeenth century. This is the earliest surviving building dating from the great period of Novgorodian architecture.

The Cathedral of St George (1119) in the Yuriev Monastery. The original roof followed the semicircular lines of the *zakomary*; the sloping roof dates from the eighteenth century.

The Cathedral of St George, Yuriev Monastery. The staircase tower and landing, with exit to the gallery. The majestic ascent of the stone spiral staircase is lit by windows at regular intervals; the walls were originally covered with frescoes, some of which are preserved in the chapel at the very top of the tower. Several deep niches to be used for private prayer were built into the staircase walls.

The Cathedral of St George, Yuriev Monastery. View of the central area from beneath the choir gallery. The beauty of this building, architecturally the finest church in Novgorod, has been somewhat spoiled by the nineteenth-century addition of stone pilasters to the medieval columns, which resulted in a narrowing of the span of the semicircular arches. The present paintings date from the 1830s.

Novgorod

In the early fifteenth century Novgorod's architectural style achieved its fullest and most distinctive development, as exemplified by the Church of St Peter and St Paul in Kozhevniki (1406), the only Novgorod church to be restored entirely to its original appearance, including its wood shingle roof and exposed red stone façades. The soaring, irregular outlines of this appealing church achieve a monumentalism which yet remains in balance with the decorative elements.

The first half of the fifteenth century witnessed a building boom in Novgorod. Nearly all the city churches – which, including those of the surrounding monasteries, amount to about one hundred and fifty – were of stone. There was much reconstruction and restoration in twelfth-century styles, and the archbishop's residence in the citadel was completed in 1433 with the Faceted Palace, built by German craftsmen.

Unfortunately only a few isolated examples of this profusion of churches have survived. Among them are two small and graceful churches, the Church of the Twelve Apostles (1454) and the Church of Lazarus (the latter known to us only in photographs). Some, such as the Church of St Simeon (1467) in the Zverin Monastery, have a two-storey structure with an extended storeroom used by the merchants who built the church, while their interiors remain traditional in appearance. In spite of the vast amount of building activity, however, little seems to have emerged in the way of new and important ideas.

The conquest of the city by Moscow between 1471 and 1478 signified the end of an independent Great Novgorod, and of a distinctive school of Novgorodian architecture. Many boyar families were forcibly transferred to Moscow, and loyal retainers sent to Novgorod in their stead.

Construction revived at the turn of the fifteenth and sixteenth centuries, when the walls and towers of the kremlin were rebuilt. A new artistic movement grew up in Novgorod which occasionally favoured traditional designs, as in the churches of St Clement (1520) and St Procopius (1529). This new style was a combination of Moscow and Novgorod traditions which produced some wholly original work. Such are the small refectory (trapezniye) churches – that is, churches incorporating a refectory at the west end – of the Antoniev and Dukhov monasteries. The ceilings of these churches are dome-shaped, and the exterior cupolas are decorated with onion domes and kokoshniki (small decorative gables). The Khutyn Monastery has an octagonal bell tower and the grandiose Cathedral of our Saviour, whose appearance and scale represent the official, state-approved architectural ethos rather than historical tradition.

This era of peaceful architectural development did not, unfortunately, last for long. Dreadful pogroms and massacres inflicted by Ivan the Terrible in 1570 had a catastrophic effect on Novgorod and were a direct cause of its dramatic decline. (On one occasion the Tsar invited all the city's boyars and clergy to a banquet, then had all the guests murdered.) The city had hardly recovered from this desolation when it was devastated anew in the early seventeenth century during the 'Time of Troubles', when Russian was wracked by civil war and a prey to foreign invaders.

The Church of St Nicholas at Lipna (1292). The first major building to be erected after the end of the period of the Mongol invasions, this church is small but impressive, with beautiful trefoil-shaped gables. The arched windows stand out clearly on the plain wall surfaces; the side windows admit light through cruciform apertures. This is the first example of the application of blind arcades to the gables as well as to the drum, a technique which reveals the influence of late Romanesque and early Baltic Gothic architecture.

Novgorod

The Church of Our Saviour of the Transfiguration on Elijah Street (1374). The original tripartite roof was replaced by the present eight-sloped roof in the sixteenth century. The façades are enlivened by a complex arrangement of windows and niches, and are carved with crosses in high relief. The circular niches were originally decorated with frescoes. The crown of the drum is the most elegant of any to be seen on Novgorod's churches.

Christ Pantocrator. Fresco on the cupola of the Church of Our Saviour of the Transfiguration (1378). This mural is by the great Byzantine artist Theophanes the Greek, who spent thirty years of his life working in Rus. It is the only work which can conclusively be ascribed to him by reference to contemporary documents. Although the mural has lost its original colours as the result of several fires, it still expresses the strength of its creator's vision. Two groups of frescoes dominate the church: on the themes of the Pantocrator in the central area, and of the Trinity in a small side-chapel in the choir. Ranked facing them are depicted groups of righteous believers – prophets, martyrs, ascetics and hermits – shown in attitudes of contemplation and prayer. (See also the three following illustrations.)

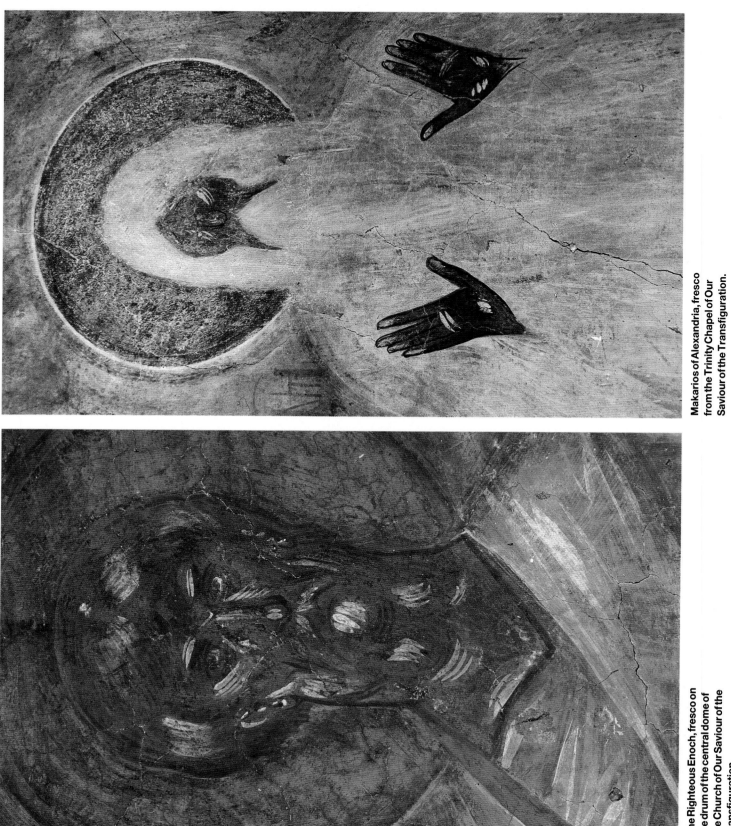

Makarios of Alexandria, fresco from the Trinity Chapel of Our Saviour of the Transfiguration.

The Righteous Enoch, fresco on the drum of the central dome of the Church of Our Saviour of the Transfiguration.

The Trinity, fresco from the
Trinity Chapel of the Church of
Our Saviour of the
Transfiguration.

After these upheavals Novgorod lost its importance as a political and artistic centre. To be sure, some marvellous churches were built in the seventeenth century, such as that for the Annunciation Monastery and two others for monasteries outside the town, the Derevyanitsky and Vyazhishchsky, but they belong to the general Russian or Moscow tradition. The refectory of the Vyazhishchsky monastery is splendidly decorated with bands and window frames of vivid green ceramic tiles.

In the eighteenth and nineteenth centuries Novgorod became a quiet provincial town of two- and three-storey stone buildings dominating a mass of low, wooden houses. At the end of the eighteenth century a drastic replanning process changed the appearance of the Sophia Side of Novgorod. The city's former glory was reduced to the status of a legend, confirmed only by its surviving architectural monuments.

During the Second World War Novgorod suffered terribly, being, by virtue of its location near Leningrad, in the front line of the three-year battle against the Germans. Practically all secular buildings, as well as churches, were severely damaged, some completely destroyed. Some monastery churches outside the city were lost forever; these included the churches of Our Saviour at Kovlyevo, the Dormition at Volotovo, St Andrew at Sitka and St Michael in Skovorotka, and St Cyril's Monastery. The Church of the Annunciation in Gorodishche and the Church of Our Saviour at Nereditsa Hill survive only partially. When the city was finally liberated in 1944, not a single civilian remained alive.

After the war the ancient monuments of Novgorod were carefully restored, but the overall appearance of the city fared less well; modern prefabricated buildings, with their alien forms and scale, destroyed much of its charm. However, the view from the River Volkhov (especially towards Lake Ilmen), as well as some parts of the Market quarter, continue to preserve the historic atmosphere of the ancient city, together with a sense of its quiet, comfortable, provincial existence a century or two ago.

Novgorod's museum possesses a marvellous collection of local art and craftsmanship. An inseparable part of the city's life is the work of the Novgorod archaeological teams, who have vividly revealed the everyday life and appearance of the city between the tenth and fifteenth centuries.

Few Russian cities can boast so rich a history, and none can compare with Novgorod in the sheer number of ancient and precious monuments.

Woods near the Yuriev Monastery. In the distance one can see the wooden, tent-roofed Church of the Dormition (1595), brought from the village of Kuritskoye and re-erected in the Museum of Wooden Architecture. This church originally housed the icon of the Dormition (see page 27).

Novgorod

The seventeenth-century Nicholas Church, originally from the village of Tukhol, now rebuilt in the Museum of Wooden Architecture. The silhouette of this simple log-constructed building was given a certain refinement with the addition of an upper section, slightly narrower at the base but widening where it meets the steep roof.

The Church of the Annunciation
at Myachino, built by Archbishop
Ioann in 1179. Its vault and part of
its façade were rebuilt in the
second half of the seventeenth
century. Inside, a series of
frescoes dating from the 1180s
has survived.

PSKOV

Pskov has long been considered Novgorod's 'younger brother'. In fact until the fourteenth century the town was under the control of Novgorod and in its cultural shadow. However, the originality of the town's structure was not affected by these factors, and the distinctive artistic style that was produced in the fourteenth century flourished well into the sixteenth. The outstanding beauty of the town's situation has found a permanent memorial in its architecture.

Pskov's location mirrors that of Novgorod in its position above a north-flowing river – the Velikaya, or Great River. Whereas Novgorod looks to the east and its kremlin stands on the west bank of the river, in Pskov, the kremlin – called the Krom – stands on the east bank, with its main defensive wall to the west. The city's position on the border of Russia (Estonia lies some fifty miles to the west) stimulated foreign trade and the diplomatic and military activity that played such a major role in its development.

The high hill on which the kremlin is built is the town's main geographical feature. The foundations date back to the tenth century, the legendary time of the Varangian Prince Igor and his Slavic wife, Princess Olga, who are said to have come from the nearby village of Bybuta. The town spreads across the Velikaya and its tributary, the Pskov, and the kremlin stands on a promontory at their confluence. From the city's earliest days, the focal point of the kremlin has been the Cathedral of the Trinity. A wooden cathedral was built in the tenth century and rebuilt in the twelfth. The present building is late seventeenth century.

Originally an outpost of Novgorod, Pskov was then ruled by that city's prince and bishop. It gained its own prince almost by chance when, in 1137, Vsevolod Mstislavich was driven out of Novgorod and came to Pskov. Pskov then became a capital city of its own region. On his death, Vsevolod was buried with great honour in the Cathedral of the Trinity.

Some Novgorod architects who came with Vsevolod were responsible for building two monastic foundations on the opposite bank of the river from the kremlin. These were the Mirozhsky Monastery and the Convent of St John (of which only the cathedral remains). Although designed by Novgorodians, the cathedrals of the monastery and convent departed from the Novgorod style in some respects. For example, the deep niches on the façades on the Cathedral of the Transfiguration of the Saviour (1156), in the Mirozhsky Monastery, clearly express its internal cruciform plan. There are no columns in the cathedral; instead the dome is supported by four interior piers at the inner corners of the crossing, clearly indicated and emphasized by painting. The lower corner bays of the building have narrow arched entrances. During the building of the western bays, concealed choir stalls were built on the first floor above ground level; these linked with the corners of the western transept.

The frescoes in the cathedral, which were begun before 1156, are strongly influenced by the Byzantine school. On entering the cathedral one sees 'The Saviour Enthroned' in the apse and, below it, the Transfiguration; in the dome there is a fresco of the Ascension. The Annunciation is painted along the walls of the central apse, and the powerful compositions of the Nativity and the Dormition of the Virgin on the east wall. The Stations of the Cross include some particularly impressive works, notably 'The Mourners at the Cross'.

Left
View of the kremlin from the point at which the River Pskov (left) joins the Velikaya (right). On the spit is a large tower from which a wooden fortification originally ran over the river to another tower on the opposite bank.

Right
View of the kremlin from the north side of the Velikaya River. It shows one of Pskov's oldest towers – the Smerdya, which dates from the fourteenth or fifteenth century. To its left the wall protects the higher part of the kremlin; to the right is the strongest section of the kremlin wall, behind which can be seen the domes of the Trinity Cathedral.

Pskov

View of the kremlin from the east. The fish market was formerly sited on the bank under the kremlin. The Trinity Cathedral dominates the city; the seventeenth-century bell tower was altered and made taller in the nineteenth century.

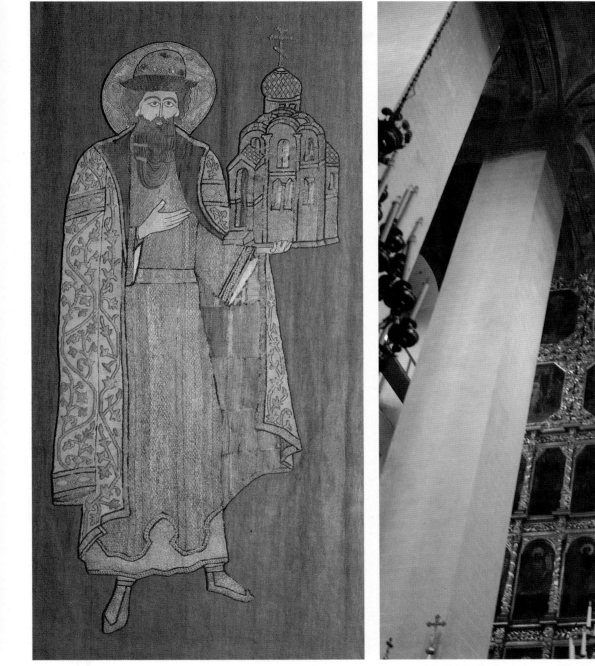

Prince Vsevolod Mstislavich holding a model of the Trinity Cathedral, nineteenth-century textile. According to tradition the cathedral was founded by Prince Vsevolod in the 1130s and, on his death, his body was brought here in 1192. The cathedral was rebuilt twice – once in the fourteenth and again in the seventeenth century.

Interior of the Trinity Cathedral. The large scale of the present building and its airy, light-filled interior are typical of contemporary city cathedrals in Russia – two other fine examples are the cathedrals of Astrakhan and Ryazan. The carved and gilded iconostasis dates from the late seventeenth century.

The Mongol invasion of 1237-42 hardly affected Pskov but as the Teutonic knights expanded their sphere of influence from the Baltic states, in 1240 Pskov briefly became a vassal of this militant order. The victory of Alexander Nevsky over the Germans at the Battle of Chudskoye Lake in 1242 (fought on the ice) returned Pskov to Russian hands.

Nevertheless, war with the German and Livonian knights continued intermittently until the late thirteenth century. Paradoxically, Livonia produced one of Pskov's greatest leaders, Prince Dovmont (died 1299), whom the town adopted as its own prince in 1266. Prince Dovmont repelled the attacks of the Teutonic knights; for more than three decades Pskov flourished, and its defences were strengthened.

In the fourteenth century the town continued to grow and prosper. An area adjoining the kremlin, called Domontov Gorod, was established. It was surrounded by stone walls, completed in the 1370s. These walls were later further extended to link with those of the Krom, and these additions were fortified with many towers.

In the fourteenth and fifteenth centuries, as the city expanded, new sections of wall – five in all – were built to contain it. More river defences were also built. The design of these fortifications reflects Pskov's new independence from Novgorod, gained in 1348. The Pskov builders constructed their walls from a combination of wood and stone. The most famous fortress was built in the village of Izborsk, near the Estonian border. At this time more than forty churches, all very skilfully designed and decorated, were built in Pskov, and the Cathedral of the Trinity was rebuilt. Stone churches were built not only in the centre, but also on the periphery. Many were constructed along the banks of the River Pskov, creating a beautiful panorama of towers and domes. By the beginning of the fourteenth century there were more than thirty monasteries and churches along the river banks.

Unfortunately, however, nearly all the churches dating from the beginning of the fourteenth century until the middle of the fifteenth have undergone alteration. The Cathedral of the Nativity of the Virgin (1310–11) in the Snetogorsky Monastery is a fine example of early Pskov architecture. It echoes the Mirozhsky Monastery's Cathedral of the Transfiguration, while maintaining its own identity. Inside the cathedral, some remarkable works of art, dating from 1313, have been preserved; the icons are sombre and expressive, yet show a light hand in their execution. Fine lines and clear, colourful pigments are applied to a dark base. The Pskov school of icon-painting was greatly admired for its bold use of colour and vigorous rhythms.

Above right
St Nicholas depicted surrounded by scenes from his life, sixteenth-century icon.

Below right
'The Descent into Hell', sixteenth-century icon.

Opposite
St Nicholas. Detail from a fifteenth-century icon from Porkhov, a small fortress to the east of Pskov. All three of these icons, now in the Pskov Museum of Art, are notable for the sense of turbulence and anxiety that they convey, which is characteristic of Pskovian painting. Despite this, the earliest, the icon of St Nicholas from Porkhov, has a gentle, lyrical quality typical of its time.

The icon of St Nicholas surrounded by scenes from his life is another good example of Pskovian painting. The scenes which form the border are comparatively large, making the central figure seem delicate and fragile. 'The Descent into Hell' has the jerky angularity we associate with fourteenth-century icons, but two new qualities characteristic of fifteenth-century icons appear: a narrative element combined with a strong sense of order, and a larger number of figures in a more formal arrangement. The colours in all three icons are characteristic, especially the dull ochre, red and earth-green: intense but thinly and unevenly applied, with a matt finish.

Left

The Cathedral of St John's Convent, second quarter of the twelfth century, opposite the kremlin, on Zavelichye, probably the work of Novgorodian builders active in Pskov. The convent was under the patronage of Pskovian princesses. The two-storey bell tower at the northwest corner dates from the sixteenth century.

Right

The Cathedral of the Transfiguration of the Saviour in the Mirozhsky Monastery, second quarter of the twelfth century. The monastery, the first and most important in Pskov, was founded by Archbishop Nifont and is built on the spit between the Velikaya and its tributary, the little River Mirozhka. A mighty dome crowns the cathedral, which is built on a cruciform plan. The bell tower is sixteenth century.

Pskov

The Pskov style of architecture is one of the most distinctive in Russia. Eschewing the pomp and grandeur characteristic of much Russian architecture in stone, the Pskov builders created churches noted for their inviting, homely, spontaneous style — yet at the same time highly ingenious in their design and construction.

These churches were normally made of rough limestone blocks, covered with plaster and whitewash. The façades, made of three flat indented planes, resembling a triptych (a feature derived from Novgorod), rise to gable roofs. The few small and discreet windows scarcely interrupt the quiet massiveness of the walls. (Occasionally these churches had to serve as fortresses.) Pillars are generally more squat than those in Novgorod; walls thicker. Yet none of these buildings appear primitive. Those of the fifteenth century are especially complex in structure, with a high central section set on a wider, lower one with its own gabled roof. With the addition of porches (a Pskov innovation of the twelfth century) and side chapels, many churches were thus endowed with a multiplicity of gables, often totalling sixteen separate slopes, which accentuate the composition in a lively manner. The recessing on the façades is echoed by inset surrounds over the windows and by similar detailing elsewhere on the building.

Pskov architects were especially known for their use of the corbelled arch. By means of superimposed arches placed over the nave at the crossing, they were able to eliminate the four piers normally required to support the drum and cupola.

Also characteristic of Pskov churches are the unusual bell gables. These are wide, flat structures, which may be small and situated on the roof of the church or several storeys high and adjacent to it. They are pierced with arched openings, each containing a bell.

Typical examples of fifteenth-century Pskov churches are the Church of Saints Cosma and Damian at Primost (1463), the Church of Saints George and Varlaam the Farmer (1495) and the wonderfully preserved Church of the Dormition in Melyotov (1462), twenty-five miles from Pskov, which is especially notable for its frescoes.

One can hardly find a better example of a fifteenth-century Pskov church than that of the Epiphany across the Pskov (1496). There used to be churches of the Epiphany on both sides of the river, but their congregations were later combined to serve the single remaining church on the further bank. At the eastern corner of the church there are two symmetrical chapels, and the northwest corner has a monumental four-arch belfry. The apses have bas-relief arches within a cylindrical cross-section which are characteristic additions of the sixteenth century.

The interior of the church is remarkably strong and powerful, its effectiveness concentrated in a fairly small space. In the west end, low, massive pillars support the choir gallery, which reflects the two-tier construction of the east wall.

Pskov's independence ended in 1510, when it was absorbed by Moscow. This event precipitated the decline of the renowned Pskov school of icon-painting, which lost its separate identity. However, it by no means hampered the development of Pskov architecture, which actually experienced something of a regeneration. Dozens of beautiful churches were built in Pskov and its environs. The most impressive of those in Pskov itself are the Church of the Dormition (1521), which has a free-standing bell tower, the Church of St Basil in Gorka, the Church of St Anastasia in Rimlyanka (1530s) and the Church of St Nicholas in Usokha (1537), reconstructed from a fourteenth-century building. The last of these has recently been restored and is now a fine example of Pskov architecture, with its satisfying asymmetrical composition and the purity of its simple interior.

Left

The Church of St Kliment (1530s), a monastery church until the eighteenth century. It has kept its original form, but the eight-sided roof and the gables were replaced in the seventeenth century by a four-sided roof and a new cross surmounting the dome. The original west porch and bell tower have not survived; the south side chapel was added in the eighteenth century.

Right

The Church of St Vasily on the Hill (1530s). Today it is surrounded by trees, but in medieval times it formed part of a large monastic complex. The stone wall of the *sredny gorod*, or middle town, ran along here from the east. Originally the church had *zakomar* gables; a two-tier gallery running round it, and side chapels at the eastern corners.

Overleaf

The Nikolsky Church on the shores of Lake Malsky (eighteenth century). Built on the site of the ancient fortress of Izborsk, which was resited in the fourteenth century and survives as New Izborsk. The original fortifications were abandoned and a number of other buildings were erected over them.

The talents of Pskov architects were already widely admired, and some of them were commissioned to work on the Moscow Kremlin. The Church of the Deposition of the Robe (1485) and the spectacular Cathedral of the Annunciation (1489) were largely the creations of Pskov architects.

With the start of the wars with the Lithuanian knights in the 1560s, building virtually ceased in Pskov. In 1571, Ivan the Terrible conducted a pogrom against the town, wiping out its entire merchant class and nobility. Ten years later the town was besieged by a Polish army of over 100,000 men. This final trial ended in the defeat of the Polish armies and peace returned to the city.

The city's cultural and economic prosperity was renewed, along with that of the whole of Russia, in the 1620s. Many new stone houses were built for the merchants and the nobility. These were two- or three-storey dwellings with room for both family and servants on the upper floors, and full basements and courtyards. Some have been preserved; most remarkable is the largest – the Pogankin House – which has recently been restored and is now a museum, containing historical and art collections.

The growth of the town and the increase in construction in stone in the seventeenth century gave Pskov a more imposing aspect. When the Cathedral of the Trinity was completed in 1699, the city attained literally new heights of grandeur. Previously, as we have noted, the churches of Pskov were relatively small, and no more grand than any large house. The cathedral, emulating the Muscovite style, rises high over the walls of the kremlin and can be seen for some fifteen miles; it has become the emblem of the town.

Although during the following century no particularly interesting buildings were constructed in Pskov, at least nothing was done to spoil its appearance. In the eighteenth and nineteenth centuries the town centre was replanned along modern lines, but the old churches were left as they were and provided a grid for the road system. Beautiful streets were now lined with both old and modern houses.

In the twentieth century Pskov suffered under the Stalinist regime, when churches were looted wholesale for museums and private 'collections', and during the Second World War it was badly damaged by German forces. Happily, however, many of its historic buildings survived. Today, Pskov is rebuilding the walls of its kremlin and is regaining something of its former beauty. In Dovmont, the medieval churches are being restored, and some treasures are being returned to their rightful places.

VLADIMIR

Once Vladimir was the capital of a mighty principality. Today, this beautiful city, set among the forests and hills of the Klyazma valley, is renowned for its gleaming white stone churches. Fortunately these twelfth-century masterpieces have not been overshadowed by the dreary functionalism of modern development. To this day they dominate the urban landscape and allow us to travel back through eight centuries to savour the glories of the city's heyday.

Vladimir was founded by Vladimir Monomakh, Grand Duke of Kiev, who built a wooden fortress here in 1108. Within fifty years it had become the powerful capital of the principality of Suzdalia with claims to be the premier city of Rus. After he became Grand Duke of Kiev in 1113 the territory was ruled first by his son Yuri Dolgoruky ('the Long-Armed'), and then, from 1157 to 1174, by Yuri's son, Andrei Bogolyubsky, who concentrated on increasing the power of Suzdalia (in the course of which he sacked Kiev and subjugated Novgorod), but who also commissioned many splendid buildings, including the royal residence at Bogolyubovo, near Vladimir.

Vladimir Monomakh chose a location for his city very similar to that of Kiev itself (even certain geographical place names

Above

The Cathedral of the Dormition (1158–1189). It was originally single-domed, and between 1185 and 1189 the addition of high galleries had the effect of enlarging the whole building. The original *zakomary* are visible from a considerable distance. Four additional domes were later added over the galleries.

Left

The Cathedral of the Dormition, apses. The vast dimensions of the cathedral and its decorative features produced a structural character similar to that of the great works of Romanesque architecture; but the downward sweep of the apses and *zakomary* still dominates the overall composition, giving the blind arcade a 'hanging' effect quite unknown in Romanesque art.

have been taken from Kiev – for example, that of the River Lybed, which borders Vladimir to the north). The important eastward route which crossed the watershed parallel to the Klyazma became Vladimir's principal thoroughfare. Between 1158 and 1164 Andrei Bogolyubsky added wooden walls on high earth ramparts to the north of the original fortress. This walled area had four gates: the Golden Gate, Irina's Gate, the Copper Gate and the Volga Gate.

To the north of Monomakh's Pecherny fortress, another fortified system, Vetchanoi, with its Silver Gate, was built around the commercial quarter. As a result Vladimir acquired a triangular plan, with development spreading along one main street and over the whole raised, wedge-shaped terrain between the Klyazma and the Lybed. The city covered 370 acres and the boundary walls were over four miles long.

At the western approach to Vladimir – that is, from the direction of the central and western Russian principalities – a road passed through the central Golden Gate. Made of oak, plated with sheets of gilded copper, the gates themselves no longer survive; but an arch within the vaulted opening of the stone ramparts marks the height of a wooden platform used by the guards who controlled the gates. The Church of the Deposition of the Robe, over the gate, was rebuilt at the beginning of the nineteenth century, when the adjoining ramparts were removed and replaced by pavilions in the neoclassical style. (The rampart to the south of the gate remained unchanged.)

The palace and church built by Yuri Dolgoruky in Vladimir (now destroyed) stood not far from the Golden Gates, on the site of the present St George's Church, which was rebuilt in the eighteenth century. Andrei Bogolyubsky concentrated his construction programme in the Pecherny district. Here the Cathedral of the Dormition was built between 1158 and 1189. It was the first church to be commissioned by Andrei and is the oldest of the city's surviving buildings. The Western European visitor is immediately struck by its close resemblance to Romanesque churches.

Unlike most of northern Russia, the area around Vladimir and Suzdal is rich in stone. Thus, instead of building churches of wood, brick or alternating bands of brick and stone, as in Kiev and Novgorod, for example, the builders of Vladimir made use of the local white limestone, exploiting its qualities with richly carved details. The clusters of pilasters, the intricately incised perspective arches of the portals, the blind arcading and the sculpture and carving – all these features recall twelfth-century Western European architecture. There is documentrary evidence that Bogolyubsky invited Frederick Barbarossa's architects and builders to work in Vladimir. Earlier, Yuri Dolgoruky had summoned his builders from Galicia, where the Polish form of Romanesque was in the ascendant.

The main distinguishing feature of Vladimir's sacred architecture was the *zakomara* – a semicircular gable crowning the walls – which was developed in eleventh-century Rus. In accordance with the accepted Byzantine principle, the centre of the building was its dome, from which movement spread downward in an even flow to integrate all the disparate elements of the church into a structural whole. This downward flow was repeated in all the arches, large and small. In the Cathedral of the Dormition, even the exterior blind arcade is of the 'hanging' type (whose effect is to enhance the downward impression). This feature is almost unknown in Romanesque architecture where the arcade always rests on some kind of plinth and thus suggests an internal gallery, whether closed or open.

The interior of the cathedral is a perfect example of the lavish and sophisticated princely art of the time. Some of the precious murals, exterior as well as interior, have been preserved. The façades were decorated with murals between the columns of the blind arcade (paintings of prophets holding scrolls have survived on the north wall); the columns, the *zakomary*, the archivolts of the portals and the dome were all dressed with gilded copper.

After a fire which damaged the city in 1185, the cathedral was rebuilt and enlarged. It was now surrounded on three sides by galleries slightly lower than the original cathedral, with the original *zakomary* projecting over the new additions; and four domes were placed at the four corners of the new building. The original exterior walls were pierced by tall arches and the three naves increased to five. These substantial changes reflected Vladimir's growing importance, placing the cathedral in the same rank as the St Sophia cathedrals of Kiev and Novgorod, and thereby strengthening Vladimir's claim to recognition as a capital city.

The royal residence at nearby Bogolyubovo (1158–65) was renowned for its splendour and luxury. It consisted of a palace and the Church of the Nativity of the Virgin, connected by galleries, surrounded by fortifications and punctuated by stair towers. One of the towers has survived, together with a gallery leading to the church and the foundations of the church itself. The ceiling of the church was supported by columns, 5 feet in diameter and crowned with carved capitals. The church was famed for its luxurious decoration, which included a lavish use of jasper, precious stones and so much gold that, according to one chronicler, it 'could not be looked upon'.

The architects of Bogolyubovo may be judged by a surviving masterpiece, the beautiful little Church of the Intercession on the Nerl, built in a single year (1165) in the flood-meadows by the bank of the Klyazma at its confluence with the Nerl, less than a mile from Bogolyubovo itself. As a precaution against floods the church was built on a high artificial hill. The foundations reached down to the base of the hill, which was paved with white flagstones; a grand stairway led up to it from the landing stage.

The Intercession has a verticality rare in Vladimir architecture. This unassertive church captures the heart with its elegant, lyrical quality. The sculpture – lions, masks and, high up in the central *zakomara*, David playing the lyre – lend a naive charm to the graceful architecture.

The interior is notable for its intimacy and, at the same time, its soaring height. A sense of harmony is created by the simplicity of the plan and the balanced distribution of light (thus avoiding extremes of light and dark) through the twenty-two windows set at various levels.

The sophistication of Vladimir art testifies to the power and authority of its rulers, but the city did endure periods of bitter struggle between ruler and nobles. In Novgorod such conflict ended with victory for the boyars. In Vladimir it was ducal power that eventually triumphed. However, Andrei Bogolyubsky paid for his despotism with his life when, in 1174, he was murdered in his own palace at Bogolyubovo by a group of conspirators. During the reign of Andrei's brother, Vsevolod III (1176-1212), the power of the nobility was decisively contained.

Vladimir

A group of the Righteous from
'The Last Judgement': fresco in
the Cathedral of the Dormition
by Andrei Rublev, c. 1408. These
frescoes are the only works
authenticated by contemporary
documents as being the work of
the master himself. The group of
figures, with St Peter at their
head, is notable for an
extraordinary sense of
expectancy and spiritual
excitement. The inscription
above – Rublev's own
description of the scene –
perfectly catches the mood:
'The Saints on their Way to
Paradise'.

'Our Lady of Vladimir', icon, early
fifteenth century. At the end of
the fourteenth century the
celebrated twelfth-century
Byzantine icon, 'Our Lady of
Tenderness', which had been
kept in the Cathedral of the
Dormition in Vladimir for two
hundred years, was transferred
to Moscow. In its place a so-
called 'reserve' (*zapasnaya*) icon
was painted, probably by Andrei
Rublev. It closely follows the
iconography of the earlier work
but differs from the original in its
lucidity, its sense of inner peace
and profound meditation, and in
the flowing style of the painting
technique, qualities uniquely
associated with Rublev. It is now
kept in the Vladimir Museum of
Art.

The Dmitrievsky Cathedral (1197). The cathedral is the most harmonious of all the works of Vladimir-Suzdal architecture. Its façades are covered with superb carving and its lavish style reflects the taste of the Grand Ducal court. Indeed, Vsevolod's palace stood next to the cathedral.

The Dmitrievsky Cathedral, interior. The proportions, unity and luminosity create a majestic impression. The limestone capitals are typical of an overall precision and perfection of form.

Vladimir

Under Vsevolod, Vladimir reached the zenith of its power and prestige. Following the reconstruction of the Dormition in 1185–89, the Dmitrievsky Cathedral (1194–97) was built not far away, next to Vsevolod's palace. In this regal church a sense of ceremony, harmony and balance is achieved by a combination of masterful proportions and flowing rhythm. The façades are light and elegantly festive. Figures of saints stand among the carved pilasters of the blind arcade: the relief carvings which cover the upper part of the building like a fine brocade incorporate floral patterns (representing paradise) and fauna (symbolizing the animal world glorifying God). Those in the *zakomary* represent such subjects as the ascension of Alexander of Macedon, Vsevolod with his sons, and David with his sling. Many of these reliefs have been restored and some have been rearranged, but those on the cupola and on the western section of the north façade are largely intact and well preserved. The interior of the cathedral is imbued with majesty and light. The columns bear carved capitals of lions. The fresco on the vaults under the choir consists of scenes from the Last Judgement. Partly painted by artists of the Constantinople school, this work is notable for the spiritual profundity, discipline and nobility of its figures and its stylistic sophistication, especially in the depiction of the Apostles and angels on the south side of the central vault. The Apostles, holding the Scriptures, are engaged in preaching and exhortation. They do not appear to condemn the supplicating sinners but, rather, to act as guarding and inspirational participants in this great drama. The atmosphere of spiritual tension was an integral part of a culture that, at first glance, might strike one as mainly festive and decorative. We are reminded that one of the inspirations of this culture was the deeply moving Byzantine icon of 'Our Lady of Tenderness', which was brought to Kiev and later secretly taken to Vladimir by Andrei Bogolyubsky. Widely known as 'Our Lady of Vladimir', it is now kept in the Tretyakov Gallery in Moscow.

Construction in early thirteenth-century Vladimir continued at a fast rate, with the archbishop's *artel* working in concert with that of the duke to erect the cathedrals of the Nativity Monastery and Knyaginin Convent.

The devastation of Vladimir in 1238 by Mongol hordes led by Batu Khan, grandson of Genghis, and the massacre of its people, were followed by more than two centuries of oppression, which drained the lifeblood from a once-flourishing culture. It was never to recover its former energy. Eventually Moscow arrogated to itself the role of political centre, although the metropolitan's *kafedra*, or seat, remained in Vladimir until the 1420s. Such was the power of tradition and the beauty of the Cathedral of the Dormition that until 1432, well after the rise of Moscow, the coronations of Russian grand dukes continued to be celebrated there.

In 1408, when it was decided to replace the cathedral's frescoes, the finest artistic *artel* Moscow could provide was dispatched to Vladimir. Its leading figure was the genius Andrei Rublev (c.1360–c.1430). Today the Cathedral of the Dormition is the only surviving church containing original works indisputably ascribed to Rublev himself.

The best preserved of these works are the sections of the Last Judgement on the vaults and arches under the choir gallery. The frescoes are a perfect example of the way in which architecture and painting can work together to unite the congregation with the holy figures around them. The Apostles and angels impress us with their sanctity – above all, perhaps, with their air of quiet contemplation. Line, the foremost element of Rublev's idiom, is free of the nervous movements typical of fourteenth-century painting but rich in its flow and uninterrupted sense of movement. Rublev's mastery of line creates both the harmony with which the whole composition is imbued and also the vivid individuality of each detail.

**Detail of a portal of the
Dmitrievsky Cathedral.**

The cathedral's original tall iconostasis, painted at approximately this time by artists from Rublev's studio, survived until 1774, when it was replaced by a new carved and gilded baroque iconostasis. The ancient icons are now kept in the Tretyakov Gallery in Moscow and the Russian Museum in Leningrad. When the icon of 'Our Lady of Vladimir' was transferred to Moscow in the early fifteenth century, a copy was made (for the Dormition in Vladimir) which is often ascribed to Rublev himself. This copy is now on display in the Vladimir Musuem of Art.

It was Vladimir's Cathedral of the Dormition that inspired the design of Aristotle Fioravanti's Dormition Cathedral (1475-79) in the Moscow Kremlin. (In fact, Fioravanti so admired the Vladimir cathedral that he said it could have been designed by an Italian.) The salient features of both cathedrals – smooth façades crowned with *zakomary* and articulated with pilasters and blind arcading; perspective arches at the portals; and the five cupolas – were repeated in many other Russian churches built in the sixteenth century. The popularity of the design, amounting almost to canonical approval, endured into the nineteenth century.

Vladimir continued to develop slowly and unremarkably between the sixteenth and eighteenth centuries. Old churches were restored and new ones, strongly influenced by the architecture of Moscow, were built. A striking early sixteenth-century example is the Dormition Cathedral of the Knyaginin Monastery, with its rising mass of *zakomary* and *kokoshniki* under a windowed dome. In the 1640s the cathedral was decorated with a magnificent mural, the huge Last Judgement, very typical of the time, which occupies the entire west wall; the side walls depict scenes from the life of the Virgin Mary.

The later Church of the Dormition of the Virgin (1649), whose construction was financed by rich merchants, greatly enhanced Vladimir's riverine panorama. Its slender form is crowned with rows of *kokoshniki*, together with the highly expressive silhouette created by its five domes. A tent-roofed bell tower adjoins the west side of the church, and there is a porch on the south side.

An intensive building programme was carried out in the eighteenth century, when the medieval layout of the town was somewhat regularized. Two twelfth-century churches, those of St George and the Holy Saviour were restored, and the charming and elegant churches of the Assumption (*Vosnesenskaya*, 1724) and St Nikola (1732-1735) were built in the hills south of the Dormition Cathedral. In additon, the high baroque Church of St Nikita (1762-65) was built on the northern edge of the city. The neoclassical period saw the construction of a group of official buildings in a style typical of provincial capitals at the time. Administrative offices (late eighteenth century) were sited between the Dormition and Dmitri cathedrals; the Assembly of the Nobility (1826), a boys' grammar school (1841) and market areas were ranged along the main thoroughfare.

The new bell tower (1810) of the Dormition Cathedral had a significant effect on the city centre. Following the fashion of the time, the architects incorporated neo-gothic and pseudo-medieval features. The tower's imposing silhouette and grand scale, accentuated by the high gilded spire, made it the dominant feature of the nineteenth-century central ensemble, whose old and new buildings it somehow drew together into an integrated whole. In 1862, however, the bell tower's effectiveness was weakened when the heavy so-called 'Russian-style' St George's Chapel was interposed between it and the Dormition Cathedral.

In our century building has continued on the edge of the medieval city and in the outlying villages, but the centre has fortunately been spared any inappropriate intrusions. Today Vladimir is protected by a special plan, sanctioned by those charged with the city's restoration, whose principal aim is the preservation of the historical and artistic heritage. Vladimir has become an international tourist centre, a fact that should determine its future development and architecture.

The Dmitrievsky Cathedral, blind arcade. The Apostles, Saints and Prophets are here shown in relief, rather than in fresco (as in the earlier Cathedral of the Dormition). The sculptural decoration of exteriors reached its apogee during the 1230s in the beautiful façades of Yuriev-Polsky's Georgievsky Cathedral, which are completely covered in carving.

Vladimir

The Church of the Intercession on the Nerl (1165). This small church is on the flood-meadows near the point where the Nerl flows into the Klyazma. It was built on an artificial hill to protect it from flood damage. The hill, which was faced with white stone, had a formal staircase leading down to the water. The church's wonderfully slender, almost fragile contours give it a delicate and highly individual appearance. It was originally surrounded by an arched gallery, whose northwest corner contained a stairway giving access to the choir gallery.

Vladimir

SUZDAL

Above

'Our Lady of Tenderness'. Icon from the first half of the fifteenth century. The dark colours lack the dramatic intensity of fourteenth-century icons, although the more open treatment gives the figures a sense of spontaneity as well as a certain emotional charge.

Left

The two monasteries facing each other across the Kamenka River, the Holy Saviour of St Yefim on the high bank and the Pokrovsky on the meadow side, make up one of the finest architectural landscapes of ancient Rus. This photograph, taken from the bell tower of the Monastery of the Holy Saviour of St Yefim, looks across to the white buildings of the Pokrovsky Monastery.

Suzdal is one of the best-known Russian cities, both at home and abroad. This familiarity is due partly to the excellent state in which so many of its monuments have been preserved and partly to its historical importance. Another reason for its popularity is the natural, comfortable way it nestles into the meanderings of the Kamenka River, in perfect accord with the contours of the surrounding landscape. Small, elegant, single- or five-domed churches and tent-roofed bell towers rise over the one- and two-storey houses, disposed randomly around the town. The panorama charms the visitor with its promise of hospitality and its subtle and complex rhythms.

However seduced we may be by the town's inviting aspect, we shall grasp its true significance only by discovering its superb works of art – especially the monumental sixteenth-century monastic ensembles and the principal cathedral, that of the Nativity of the Virgin, which dates from the era of lavish royal patronage just before the Mongol invasions.

Suzdal is more than a thousand years old. In ancient times the name applied not to a town but to the whole area; the first mention we have of it is in an eleventh-century manuscript. Several small settlements occupied the site of present-day Suzdal, which was situated in the midst of an *opolya*, a fertile, treeless plain, set – by some quirk of nature – among the dense forests that covered the region in the eleventh and twelfth centuries. Its metamorphosis into a city is associated with the rule of Vladimir Monomakh (1113-25). He threw a rampart around one bend of the river and constructed a wooden fortress, within which the original brick-and-stone Church of the Nativity of the Virgin was built.

When Vladimir's son, Yuri Dolgoruky (1149-57) became ruler of Suzdalia he built a royal residence at Kidekshe-by-Suzdal on the River Nerl. There, in 1152-57, he erected the Church of St Boris and St Gleb, one of the earliest examples of the distinctive Vladimir-Suzdal architectural school. The sober, smooth walls of white stone are softened by twin and triple rows of pilasters, portals, *zakomary* and arched concentric window surrounds. The façades are decorated with blind arcading running around the entire building – the first local example of this embellishment.

During the reign of Andrei Bogolyubsky, the political and creative life of the principality of Suzdalia was concentrated in Vladimir, which also became the centre of architectural activity. Large-scale construction resumed in Suzdal only in the early thirteenth century, when the son of Vsevolod III, Yuri Vsevolodovich, replaced the old cathedral with a new one, built of limestone. The size and grandeur of the new building testifies to Suzdal's increased significance at this time. Such an imposing architectural presence implies a highly developed urban culture.

Barely half of this second cathedral has survived. When the upper section was rebuilt in 1528-30, the architects preserved the scale and, to some extent, the forms of the old cathedral, although they replaced the original three domes with the five-domed design now required by canon law and added three transepts. Built of slabs of tufa, these are richly embellished, around the portals, with carvings in stone. The western transept is two storeyed and led to the

The Cathedral of the Nativity of the Virgin (1222–1225, 1528–1530). Its scale and opulence, and its position at the centre of the kremlin next to the Archbishop's Palace (built between the sixteenth and eighteenth centuries), make it the architectural focus of the whole city. The original three domes were replaced in the sixteenth century by the five we see today. The cathedral's interior is a museum in itself; its treasures include outstanding frescoes dating from the 1230s and the 1630s; a late seventeenth-century gilded *tyablovy* iconostasis (an iconastasis the icons of which are painted directly onto wooden boards); the painted screen, or *sorochka*, behind the iconostasis; a remarkable chandelier; the canopy over the throne; and the earliest bronze doors in Russia, with designs executed in gold on a black background by means of a technique known as fired gilding.

Suzdal

Views of the Monastery of the Holy Saviour of St Yefim from the River Kamenka. The Kamenka makes a 180-degree turn here; in its oxbow nestles the Pokrovsky Monastery, with the walls and towers, domes and tent roofs of the Monastery of the Holy Saviour of St Yefim rising above it. The photograph on the right shows the monastery domes and the tent roof of the refectory church beyond the walls; to the right the octagonal corner tower and the great square entrance tower, with the Church of the Annunciation over the gates. The photograph on the left shows the cathedral and refectory.

Suzdal

Left
**The Cathedral of the
Transfiguration in the
Monastery of the Holy Saviour of
St Yefim. The little single-domed
church in the foreground was the
monastery's first stone
'cathedral', built in 1509 over the**

tomb of the founder, Father
Yefim. It has an unusual two-part
division of the façades and,
inside, a vaulted ceiling
unsupported by columns.
Following the construction of
the huge five-domed cathedral
in the late sixteenth century, the

original building was converted
into a side church.

Above
The central ensemble of the
Monastery of the Holy Saviour of
St Yefim. Left, the Dormition
refectory church (1525); centre,

the cathedral (sixteenth
century); right, the octagonal
bell tower dating from the first
half of the sixteenth century,
with another building, added in
1691, adjoining it.

choir stalls, which occupied the entire west end of the building.

The cathedral presents a somewhat austere appearance, apart from its star-spangled blue onion domes, with the simple façades elegantly relieved by sparely applied architectural details. As the spiritual focus of the city, as a whole, it required a treatment very different from that of the elaborately decorated royal cathedrals, such as the Dmitrievsky in Vladimir or the Georgievsky in Yurev-Polsky. This restraint was not for lack of means, for the cathedral interior was richly endowed. The splendid western and southern gates (thirteenth-century) have survived; they are faced with copper sheets, which were etched and gilded. The western gate bears scenes from the life of Christ and of the Virgin; the southern, episodes involving the archangels.

During the fourteenth century, Suzdal led the struggle against the rising power of Moscow — a struggle that was doomed to failure. In 1392 it was annexed by Moscow, and its political significance dwindled rapidly. It continued to be an important religious centre: small monasteries and convents were established along the Kamenka River above and below the city. These included, to the north, the Rizpolozhensky, the Alexandrovsky, the Intercession and the Holy Saviour of St Yefim; and to the west, the Vasily and other monasteries. However, the city's meagre economic resources caused, in time, an architectural stagnation. When the upper part of the Cathedral of the Nativity of the Virgin collapsed in 1445, there was neither the means nor the will to rebuild it, and within eighty years it was in ruins.

Suzdal's artistic revival in the early sixteenth century was due to the rulers of Muscovy, who were prepared to pour money into the city and rebuild the monasteries. In 1510 Grand Duke Vasily III (1505-33) commissioned Moscow architects to construct the Cathedral of the Intercession in the convent of the same name, together with the Holy Gate and the Church of the Annunciation above it. The dedication of these buildings, like that of the rebuilt Refectory and Church of the Immaculate Conception, was inspired by the hope of curing the apparent barrenness of Vasily's wife, the Grand Duchess Solomonia Saburova, who had been unable to provide the dynasty with an heir. It was to this convent that Solomonia was forcibly exiled in 1525. Members of other notable families — including Eudoxia, the first wife of Peter the Great — were detained there in the seventeenth and eighteenth centuries.

The Cathedral of the Intercession (1518), although somewhat austere in appearance, has a certain gentle, rhythmic quality. It is a raised building (the ground floor contained tombs) surrounded on three sides by open galleries. The walls are crowned with keel-shaped *zakomary*. The cathedral itself has three domes, the base of the central dome being beautifully decorated with *kokoshniki*, semicircular or ogival miniature gables. The walls are relieved by blind arcading. The interior of the cathedral contained no murals; the purity of its white stone was heightened by the black tiles paving the floor.

The Gate Church of the Annunciation (1518) is distinguished by the elegance and decorative complexity of its façades. The refectory is decorated by a band of bricks arranged in rhomboid pattern (a familiar feature of northern European Gothic architecture).

The Pokrovsky Cathedral of the Pokrovsky Monastery (1518). The clear, elegant lines of the cathedral were mainly inspired by contemporary Moscow architecture, but the three-dome arrangement and unusual blind arcade derive from a Suzdal church, the Nativity of the Virgin. Note particularly the flowing nature of the design, the *kokoshniki* round the central dome, the weaving lines of the *zakomary* and the icon-niche at the centre of the façade.

Left

Ensemble comprising the Churches of St Lazarus (1667) and St Antipy (1745). A scene typical of medieval Russian cities, and especially of Suzdal, with a large summer church and a small, warm winter church. St Antipy is adjoined by a bell tower of the same period, with a concave tent roof, circular acoustic apertures and brightly painted façades. In the background is Suzdal's highest building, the bell tower of the Rizpolozhensky Monastery (the name refers to the Feast of the Deposition of the Robe), built by the citizens of Suzdal in 1819 to commemorate the defeat of Napoleon.

Right

The Church of the Resurrection, (1732). A typical example of Suzdal's parish churches. The façades are clear and uncluttered, except for the ornamentation of the socle and the lightly painted *zakomary*. To the north is the low, winter Church of the Virgin of Kazan (1739).

Suzdal

View of the Kamenka River from the Museum of Wooden Architecture on its banks. In the distance is the cruciform Church of the Transfiguration from the village of Kozlyatyevo (1756).

The Church of Saints Cosma and Damian (1725). One of the most attractive buildings in Suzdal. The ensemble consists of the main building, a side chapel with a little dome, and the elegant bell tower with a slightly concave tent roof. This picturesque

scene was originally completed
by a low stone wall and stone
steps leading down to the water.

The ensemble was completed by two bell towers crowned by tent roofs. One is by the cathedral proper (its upper part also provided access to the cathedral in the seventeenth and eighteenth centuries); the other, which originally bore a clock, is at the southwest corner of the refectory.

In the seventeenth century the convent was surrounded by a low wall set with towers. To this day the convent, standing on the lower bank of the river, seems like a magical little white city. The beauty of the setting is enhanced by the steep slopes that accompany the winding Kamenka and by the high bank opposite the convent, with the Monastery of the Holy Saviour of St Yefim towering above it.

The Monastery of the Holy Saviour of St Yefim was founded in 1352. It acquired its first stone building in 1509, when a small single-domed church was built over the tomb of the monastery's founder, Father Superior Yefim. The year 1525 saw the construction of the Refectory Church of the Dormition, one of the earliest examples of tent-roof architecture. The church has an adjoining side chapel crowned with a delicate filigree of rows of *kokoshniki*, which heighten the dynamism and strength of the entire composition. A belfry with a tent roof (similar to that in the Convent of the Intercession) was built nearby, and twice increased in size by the addition of annexes on the southern side, with the result that, by the seventeenth century, it possessed three hipped roofs.

The monastery's original Cathedral of the Transfiguration must have seemed too small for such an imposing ensemble, for it was replaced in 1594 by a new and more grandiose building. However, the old church was not demolished but became the south side chapel. The design for the new cathedral, the city's second largest building, was inspired by the country's foremost cathedral – the Dormition in Moscow – and also drew on the forms of the rebuilt Suzdal Cathedral of the Nativity of the Virgin.

In the seventeenth century the monastery was transformed into a mighty fortress, whose formidable aspect contrasts sharply with the charming countryside along the Kamenka and the open and welcoming appearance of the Convent of the Intercession.

The artistic significance of the Cathedral of the Transfiguration was enhanced in 1689 when its southern and western exterior walls were adorned with magnificent frescoes, painted by artists from the studio of two famous masters, Guri Nikitin and Sila Savin.

One other stone church was erected in the sixteenth century – in the Monastery of the Deposition of the Robe. This relatively low five-domed church has no internal columns and was evidently designed for a congregation of modest size. It indicates the revival of a preference for churches on a more intimate scale.

This intensive monastic building programme was followed by the restoration and redevelopment of the kremlin ensemble. In addition to rebuilding the Cathedral of the Nativity of the Virgin, the authorities ordered the construction of a new Archbishop's Palace to be erected next to the cathedral.

The Church of St Nicholas (1766) from the village of Glotovo. It was transferred from its original site to the Suzdal kremlin in the 1950s, to become the first exhibit of the Museum of Wooden Architecture. A simple log church, it is given significance and elegance by the addition of a high, steep roof and a hanging gallery. The museum was subsequently moved to the opposite bank of the Kamenka, by the Church of Saints Boris and Gleb (1747) which may also be seen in this photograph.

In the sixteenth century, Suzdal's *posad*, with its many wooden churches, was situated beyond the rampart to the east and north of the kremlin. Monasteries surrounded the city, so that there were a number of settlements scattered around the countryside. In 1573 Suzdal included twenty parish churches and twenty-seven monastic churches – and this in a city of barely four hundred households!

The seventeenth century did not restore Suzdal to prosperity. It suffered two Polish invasions, with their inevitable depredations which, by mid-century, had reduced the population to some three hundred households. Nevertheless, immediately after this period Suzdal architecture embarked on a new and exciting phase, partly involving the monasteries but mainly due to commissions from individual patrons. Dozens of new parish churches transformed the structure of the city by drawing the kremlin, the *posad* and the monasteries into an integrated whole.

One of these, the Church of St Lazarus, was built in the *posad* in 1667. The simplicity of its exterior walls is relieved by pilasters and a cornice under the *zakomary*. Five shapely onion domes crown the high roof.

Later designs for such churches were even lighter, more inviting and more ornamental. They are to be found in monasteries (for example, the Alexandrovsky Monastery, 1695) as well as in the *posad* (for example, the Smolensk Church, 1696-1707). Pilasters were used at corners only; exterior surfaces were light and clean, so that the sparely ornamented frames of the symmetrically arranged windows and portals on these pure façades suggest embroidery on white cloth. The *zakomary* – up to thirteen on each façade – acquired a less stark profile, becoming gradually less architectural and more ornamental in character, and sometimes even being broken off at the angle between one façade and another. The five-dome design remained the norm, but corner domes lost their windows.

The Tsar Constantine Church (1707) has typical eighteenth-century baroque cupolas – narrow, with exaggerated ornamentation and shapely silhouettes. However, Suzdal architects were now designing single-cupola churches, whose purity of line was complemented by a small number of simply arranged apertures and decorative bands. Individual features were often rendered in bright colours, such as the green and red arches on the cornice of the St Nicholas Church, built between 1720 and 1739. Simplicity and elegance, the two outstanding qualities of Suzdal churches, come together in perfect harmony in the Church of the Resurrection (1732) which stands in the centre of the market square.

All the above-mentioned churches were for summer use. The warmer wooden winter churches built next to them were gradually replaced by low stone buildings and, together with the summer churches, formed the 'pairs' we see today, such as, for example, the Church of the Lamentation (winter, 1750) by the Tsar Constantine Church (summer) and the Virgin of Kazan (winter, 1739) next to the Church of the Resurrection (summer, 1732). The small wooden churches were often crowned with tent roofs.

Windmills from the village of Drachevo in the Museum of Wooden Architecture (nineteenth century).

93

Tent roofs first appeared in Suzdal monasteries in the sixteenth century. By the early eighteenth century they were as ubiquitous a feature of the skyline as onion domes. For example, the richly decorated tent-roof Holy Gates of the Convent of the Deposition of the Robe were built in 1688; and a tent-roof bell tower, notable for its severity and purity of form, was erected next to the cathedral of the Alexandrovsky Monastery at about the same time.

A specifically Suzdalian variation of the tent-roof bell tower, which first appeared in the early sixteenth century, is the concave tent roof. The gracefully elongated lines of such bell towers (for example, those of St Lazaurus and St Nicholas) give an additional charm to the elegance of the Suzdal skyline.

The kremlin retained its dominant position even in the enlarged city, which, by the seventeenth century, embraced the monasteries as well as the *posad*, with its many churches. In 1635 Archbishop Serapion built a mighty tent-roofed bell tower to the south of the cathedral. Around the beginning of the eighteenth century Metropolitan Hilarion constructed a spacious new Archbishop's Palace which enclosed the existing sixteenth-century buildings. The main façade of the L-shaped palace, decorated with broad windows and pilastered window frames, faces the area between the cathedral and the bell tower; the main entrance to the palace was through a ceremonial porch opposite the cathedral's western annexe. The palace was a three-storeyed building with four high sloping roofs which moderated its great size and gave it a more picturesque character.

Today the palace houses the Suzdal Historical Museum, which includes an outstanding collection of icons. The fifteenth- and sixteenth-century icons are notable for their elegance and refinement of composition and their bright and festive colours. The museum also occupies part of the Holy Saviour of St Yefim Monastery, where works of thirteenth – seventeenth-century decorative and applied art are exhibited.

In the 1950s a museum of wooden architecture was established in Suzdal. Its first acquisition, now to be found in the palace courtyard, was the Church of St Nicholas (1766), brought from the village of Glotovo. This is a small building of simple log construction with a suspended gallery. A much more elaborate example is the Church of the Transfiguration (1756), from Koslyatyevo, a veritable wedding cake in wood – its three octagonal tiers liberally embellished with curved gables and delicate onion domes. The spiky silhouettes of these wooden churches, set among the greenery and the peasant log houses transferred to the site perfectly complement the grander shapes of the masonry buildings.

After several centuries as a backwater, Suzdal is now enjoying a rebirth as a busy and much-loved tourist centre. Although the urban improvement programme of the 1970s and 1980s gave the city a somewhat over-regulated appearance, it did not, fortunately, change the relaxed and measured pace of life led by its inhabitants, amid their historic heritage of superb Russian religious architecture.

Contemporary wooden house on the bank of the Kamenka. An *izba* (peasant log house) of a traditional type whose history stretches back almost a thousand years. Ordinary town and country people lived in similar houses until the nineteenth century. Rich families often built themselves much larger wooden homes, often of two storeys, especially in Northern Russia. This more modest scale is typical of Russian provincial towns in the late nineteenth century – a house with three or four windows, the front garden filled with flowers, a fence along the street and a small vegetable garden or orchard at the back.

Suzdal

ZAGORSK

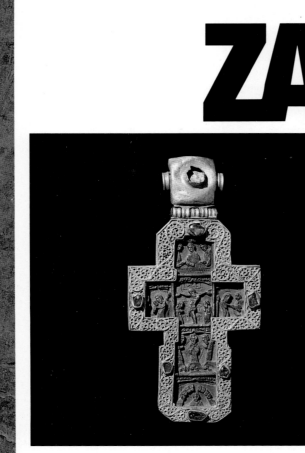

Above
Crucifix of wood, filigree and precious stones (sixteenth century).

Left
Religious procession in the Trinity-St Sergius Monastery.

The history of Zagorsk spans seven centuries, although it has been the history of a city for only the last two hundred years. Before that time it was the history of a very powerful Russian monastery, the Trinity-St Sergius *Lavra* (monastery of the highest rank), perhaps the most important spiritual centre of Russia between the fourteenth and seventeenth centuries. Until the end of the eighteenth century the monastery held sway over its outlying districts and the *posad*, or market quarter; but then the *posad* became a city in its own right. It existed under the name of Sergiev for some one hundred and fifty years until its latest change of name, in 1930, to Zagorsk (after a revolutionary killed by an anarchist in 1919).

Even in the nineteenth century the monastery continued to exert considerable influence over the city. The monastery was the town's architectural centre, a kind of citadel or kremlin, and even today Zagorsk is almost totally identified with the Trinity-St Sergius *Lavra*. This is a little unfair; from the eighteenth century onwards some other interesting buildings, both religious and secular, sprang up near the monastery. Nevertheless it is the striking view of the *Lavra* that is the main attraction for artists and tourists alike.

The monastery was founded by the renowned Russian national hero, zealot and ascetic Sergius Radonezhsky (1322-92). Christened Barfolomei, he was born in Rostov to an impoverished boyar family who later moved to the small town of Radonezh, near Moscow. After the death of his parents, Barfolomei and his brother, Stefan, resolved to take monastic orders and become hermits in the forest. About six miles north of Radonezh they found a clearing on Makovets Hill, where they built a cell and the small Trinity Church (c. 1345).

Stefan soon left his brother for the Bogoyavlensky Monastery in Moscow; after taking his vows Barfolomei assumed the name of Sergius and continued his solitary life. His holiness and good works attracted followers, who joined forces with him in 1355 to found a strict monastery of their own. By the 1360s it had acquired the layout typical of Russian and Greek monasteries—that is, a church (the Trinity) surrounded on all four sides by the monks' cells.

The ascetic and spiritual way of life led by the monks soon gained the respect of Sergius' contemporaries. He and his disciples founded more than twenty other monasteries in the second half of the fourteenth century. His appeal to his countrymen to put aside feudal dissension and unite under the leadership of Moscow to shake off Tatar rule found a powerful response. Sergius' blessing was of the greatest moral and political support to Grand Duke Dmitri Donskoy, who in 1380 defeated the Tatar forces in the battle of Kulikovo.

This victory did not, however, bring final liberation to Russia. The campaign of Tokhtamysh (1382) and other Tatar incursions continued to devastate the country. In 1408 the Trinity Monastery itself was razed to the ground. By 1412, however, it had been rebuilt. Ten years later, by order of Father Nikon, a disciple of Sergius, the original wooden Trinity Cathedral was transported eastwards. Construction of a new white limestone cathedral was begun over the tomb of Sergius, who had by now been proclaimed a patron saint of Russia.

The new Trinity Cathedral (1423) is an outstanding example of fifteenth-century Moscow church architecture, a perfect blend of the severity appropriate to a monastery and the elegant and refined forms identified with the capital and the court. The few small windows

emphasize its massive solidity, while the noticeable declivity of the walls and drum gives it a rather mausoleum-like appearance. Its purity of form, the beauty of the horizontal bands of carving on the façades, the apses and the dome, and the striking *zakomary* all reveal an elevated taste. In spite of the many changes that the monastery experienced in the ensuing centuries, the Trinity Cathedral remained its undisputed centre; this status was confirmed in the mid-sixteenth century by the gilding of the cupola, and again in the eighteenth century, when the whole roof was gilded.

The visitor entering the cathedral is immediately struck by the atmosphere of spiritual contemplation. Arches and graduated vaults lead the eye up through the dark interior towards the light of the drum high overhead.

The cathedral's original murals were replaced in 1635 by frescoes, some of which survive high up on the walls and in the vaults. The lower four rows of the iconostasis date from the 1420s (the fifth, 'Church Fathers', row was added in the sixteenth century). The icons of the lowest three rows are the work of painters from the studio of Andrei Rublev. The combination of harmony and strength expressed in the figure of the Apostle Paul is reminiscent of the style of Rublev himself, and the icons of the feast-day row, especially 'The Feast of Purification', 'The Washing of Christ's Feet', 'The Eucharist' and 'The Three Marys at the Tomb of Christ' are particularly notable for their subtly lyrical and deeply devotional qualities. The iconostasis contains a copy of Rublev's 'Trinity' icon, which was presented to the monastery by Ivan IV, the Terrible.

Today the original is in the Tretyakov Gallery in Moscow. The original Royal Doors (1643) of the iconostasis are on display in the monastery's museum.

The lower 'local' row of the iconostasis, to the left, contains another copy of the 'Trinity', this one dating from the late sixteenth century. Tsar Boris Godunov (1598-1605) transferred the original jewelled frame (commissioned by Ivan the Terrible) from Rublev's 'Trinity' onto this copy and replaced it with another one; today both of these frames are on show in the museum.

Two of the icons from the Trinity iconostasis, 'The Saviour Not Made With Hands' (also known as the Vernicle, or veronica) and 'The Saviour on the Throne', dating from 1674 and 1684 respectively, are the work of another celebrated icon painter, Simon Ushakov (1626-86). To the right of the iconostasis, by the south wall, candles burn day and night while prayers are intoned over the tomb of St Sergius, a silver sarcophagus in the mid-sixteenth century, to which a canopy was added in the eighteenth century.

The Trinity-St Sergius Monastery taken from the southeast, the view which best conveys the architectural, historical and cultural richness, as well as the artistic unity, of the ensemble. The mighty domes of the Cathedral of the Dormition and the great baroque bell tower with its gilded corona dominate the skyline. To the left is the Sergiev Church; beyond the great Pyatnitsa corner tower we see the five elegant golden domes of the Church of John the Baptist over the gates; on the extreme right, the Krasnaya entrance tower. In front of the walls: left, the Pyatnitsa Church and the Church of the Presentation of the Virgin; centre, the Chapel of St Pyatnitsa's Well.

Left

The gallery set into the wall of the Trinity-St Sergius Monastery. It runs along the walls, across all twelve towers.

Right

The walls and Sushilnaya Tower of the Trinity-St Sergius Monastery (sixteenth and seventeeth century). The two projecting galleries along the walls date from the two periods in the seventeenth century when the old walls were doubled in height.

Zagorsk

The Trinity Monastery grew rapidly, thanks largely to munificent donations from grand dukes and other nobility. In 1469 a stone refectory and kitchen (neither of which has survived) were built to the north of the cathedral. In 1476 a new brick church, that of the Descent of the Holy Spirit, was built on the site of the old wooden cathedral. The work of Pskov craftsmen, it is an example of the sophisticated Moscow style of church-building, which Pskov architects had largely created. The façades of this elegantly proportioned church are articulated by clusters of pilasters and attached columns, and enlivened by a decorative band of incised zigzags over balusters, set between two scrollwork friezes, and by a rhythmical line of keel-shaped *zakomary*. The apses are ornamented with small attached columns which appear to be suspended from a large swagged garland.

The Church of the Descent of the Holy Spirit is a rare example of a church 'under the bells'; its single dome sits on a hexagonal arched belfry.

The sixteenth century brought additions on a different scale, in keeping with the monastery's growing economic power. The ancient road to Vologda was now part of the trade route to Europe, and the former backwater suddenly bubbled with life. The monastic lands were greatly extended northwards and eastwards; steep hills limited expansion in other directions. As a result, the Cathedral of the Trinity, formerly at the centre of the architectural ensemble, now gave the appearance of having been transposed to the southwest corner of the composition. New brick walls, in an irregular rectangle about a mile long, were constructed in the 1540s and fortified with twelve towers; extra protection was provided on the south side by a stretch of water. A gated tower, crowned by the Church of St Sergius (now replaced by that of St John the Baptist), was built on the eastern side, which was additionally fortified by a dry moat.

In 1548 a side chapel was added to the south side of the Trinity Cathedral to accommodate the tomb of Father Nikon; and in 1547 two stone churches, the Presentation of the Virgin and the Pyatnitsky (dedicated to St Paraskeva Pyatnitsa), were built outside the monastery proper at the foot of the hill.

The principal new building of the period, however, was the Cathedral of the Dormition (1559-85). It was placed at the centre of the newly extended territory and henceforward dominated the whole ensemble. Its air of authority, derived from the disciplined arrangement of its constituent parts, together with its massive scale, recall its namesake in the Moscow Kremlin. The bodies of Boris Godunov, his wife and two of his children lie buried just outside the cathedral's west door.

The cathedral's dominant position is augmented by the gradual upward slope of the land to the east of the Trinity Cathedral. The four churches – the Trinity, the Descent of the Holy Spirit, the Dormition and St Sergius above the Gate – formed the majestic skyline of the monastery as it was seen from the Moscow road. The formidable red brick walls, framing the white churches and the wooden buildings, eloquently conveyed the monastery's other role, as a fortress.

The three principal architectural eras of the Trinity-St Sergius Monastery are represented in this photograph. The fine Church of the Descent of the Holy Spirit (1476), on the left, displays the subtlety, precise contours, sophistication and harmony of proportion characteristic of early Moscow court architecture. The Cathedral of the Dormition, on the right, with the measured regularity of its massive forms, displays the official, state-dominated style associated with the reign of Ivan the Terrible. The soaring baroque bell tower, in the centre, on the north side of the monastery square, became the dominant vertical element of the monastery in the eighteenth century.

The Trinity Cathedral (1427), the earliest and most important element of the monastery. It houses the tomb of St Sergius Radonezhsky. The Nikolsky chapel on the south side was built in 1548 over the tomb of Father Nikon, Sergius's successor. Recent work has returned the roof to its original beauty (except for the *kokoshniki* round the base of the drum, which have not yet been restored).

Interior of the Trinity Cathedral, an architectural and spiritual masterpiece of Russian medieval art. The dim light of the lower areas emphasizes the importance of the central space, lit by the windows of the dome. The high iconostasis, the oldest in Rus, is attributed to the studio of Andrei Rublev; the silver tomb of St Sergius (with elements dating from the sixteenth, eighteenth and nineteenth centuries) stands in front of the south end.

The Church of the Descent of the
Holy Spirit (1476). A very unusual
design; a belfry was built at the
base of the drum.

The Church of Our Lady of
Smolensk (1748). The building is
circular in plan, the circle being
transformed into a cruciform
structure by the device of
concave niches. The axes of this
structure are accentuated by
stairways, broken pediments
and dormers. The capitals of the
twinned pilasters and the
mouldings under the windows
are without ornament.

Infirmary wards and the Church of Zosima and Savvaty (1637). The infirmary consisted of several buildings with high roofs; the centre of the complex was an open court with an ornate tent-roofed church and a staircase leading to it. The apse repeats the ornamentation of the Church of the Descent of the Holy Spirit. Green tiles decorate the high tent roof, which is separated from the main body of the church by a windowless passage.

Zagorsk

The early seventeenth century was a time of great trials for the monastery. Between 1608 and 1610, during the Time of Troubles, it valiantly withstood a sixteen-month siege by Polish invaders. After a final attempt by the Poles to take the monastery failed in 1618, a peace treaty marking the end of such incursions was signed in the nearby village of Deulino.

The monastery's power and influence continued to grow, its lands were further extended, and great riches, in the form of offerings and donations, added to its wealth and financed much new building. The thickness and height of the walls were doubled, and an infirmary and the neighbouring tent-roofed Church of Saints Zosima and Savvaty (1635-37) were added to the row of cells on the west side. Although the monastery walls were now whitewashed, the churches themselves gradually became more colourful. The slender tent roof and the façades of the infirmary church were faced with green tiles; and murals were painted on the *zakomary* of the Dormition and, somewhat later, on those of the Trinity Cathedral.

Peter the Great (1682-1725) twice took refuge in the monastery; in 1682, fleeing from a rebellion by the *streltsi* (members of a privileged military corps), and in 1689, during his struggle for power with the Empress Sophia. The Petrine era brought to the monastery the colourful, festive style known as Moscow, or Naryshkin, baroque. This is a fusion of Western baroque motifs and Russian forms, typically incorporating tiers and rows of *kokoshniki*. The new Chertogi Palace (1690s) and a spacious refectory (1686-92) were built in this style, by the south and north walls, to replace the old wooden palaces.

The refectory is set on a broad ground storey and flanked on the north side by a graceful porch. The façades are articulated by attached columns, and the slender carved spiral columns framing the windows bear curved pediments containing small icons. Above the cornice is a row of large concave shell motifs – a popular design adapted from Western baroque. The main part of the façades is painted in a pattern of dark blue, red and green to create a trompe l'oeil faceted effect.

The Chertogi Palace, where the tsar stayed when visiting the monastery, was built immediately after the refectory – and evidently by the same architects. Rows of paired windows are the principal architectural motif of the two-storey façades. On the lower floor the window frames are relatively simple, but those of the first floor are elaborately carved and set with ceramic tiles. The walls are painted similarly to those of the refectory, with tiles in the cornices and larger tiles mounted higher up. Originally these buildings had two wide front porches with steps leading from ground level to the first floor. The decor inside dates from the second half of the eighteenth century.

Another example of late seventeenth-century baroque is the graceful single-domed Chuch of St John the Baptist, also called the Church over the Gates, built between 1693 and 1699 to replace the earlier St Sergius Church. The baroque cupola was added in 1746.

These ornate and colourful new buildings give the monastery a festive air, which nevertheless harmonizes with the elegance of the fifteenth-century Trinity Cathedral and the solemnity of the Dormition. The same spirit is evident in the little chapel built over a well by the southwest corner of the Dormition Cathedral; its exterior is bright and colourful, decorated with tracery and cartouches.

Refectory hall (1692). The largest late seventeenth-century refectory in existence, it adjoins the Chertogi Palace. The present décor dates from the end of the eighteenth century.

The unusual superstructure on the northeast Utichya Tower, probably dating from the late seventeenth century, is directly derived from Dutch models (notably the Rathuis in Maastricht). In the eighteenth century the Church of Our Lady of Smolensk (1746-48) added a more sophisticated version of baroque, in the style of a palatial pavilion, to the monastery. The Kalichya (Pilgrim) Tower in the northwest corner of the walls was rebuilt in 1778 and enhanced by a high tent roof. At the same time the upper parts of the other towers were altered and given cupolas with spires, which may still be seen on the north and east sides of the monastery.

By 1744, when the monastery achieved the status of *Lavra*, its composition and silhouette had become so complex that a new unifying element was required. This was provided in the form of a marvellous bell tower, the finest in eighteenth-century Russia. Building on the tower continued from 1740 to 1770. The original design, proposed by I. Schumacher, called for a three-tiered structure, to be situated opposite the western entrance to the Dormition Cathedral. With the building already under construction two prominent architects, I. Michurin and Prince Dmitri Ukhtomsky, had it transferred to a new site and rebuilt with five tiers topped by an ornate gold crown under the cross. Thanks to their intuition and the height of the tower – nearly 300 feet – this light, traceried building perfectly completed the composition of the monastery, by then four hundred years in the making. From the massive cube at the base of the tower the upper tiers ascend with increasing delicacy, incorporating – in the best baroque manner – classical as well as more fanciful features.

The nineteenth century brought only some changes for the worse. In 1814 the formal porches of the Chertogi Palace were demolished when the Moscow Theological College took over the building; and when the Krassnaya Tower was rebuilt in 1856 the dull and derivative design of the façades and top spoilt the main entrance to the monastery itself.

After the Revolution of 1917 the monastery's importance, far from diminishing, actually increased. All through the years of official repression of the church it continued to function as one of the holy and inviolate places of Russia.

Since 1920 the *Lavra* has contained a Museum of Art and History, whose collections are based on the monastery's own extraordinarily rich fund of treasures gathered over the centuries. Pride of place must go to the collection of old Russian paintings, which also includes the frescoes and iconostases that remain in the monastery churches. Also outstanding are the murals and huge carved and gilded iconostasis (1688) of the Dormition Cathedral, and the iconostasis from Moscow's Church of St Paraskeva Pyatnitsa, now in the Smolensk Church. The icon section includes two wonderful paintings of the Virgin dating from the fourteenth and fifteenth centuries, 'The Virgin Hodegetria' and 'The Virgin Perivlepta', 'St Anna with Mary', 'St Nikola' (the personal icon of Sergius Radonezhsky) and many others.

The jewellery collection displays some of the lavish gifts received by the monastery, as well as works by the monastery's own craftsmen – for example, excellent small carved wooden icons from the fifteenth-century studio of Amfrosii. Liturgical vessels from the fifteenth, sixteenth and seventeenth centuries are particularly sumptuous.

Masterpieces of Old Russian embroidery are also on display. The funeral pall of St Sergius (1420s) with its highly individual, portrait-like representation of the saint, is an outstanding work by craftsmen who may well have seen Sergius themselves. A shroud of 1499, with paintings of Golgotha and various saints and festivals, was presented to the monastery by the Muscovite Grand Duchess Sophia Paleologue. Another gift, presented by Grand Duke Vasily III and his wife Solomonia Saburova, in the hope that they would be rewarded by the birth of a male heir, is a similar shroud of 1525 depicting the appearance of the Virgin to Sergius.

The Trinity-Sergius *Lavra* is no less richly endowed and important than the Moscow Kremlin itself. It has a special additional value in its continuing significance as a spiritual centre of the Russian nation. The restoration of many of the buildings during the 1950s and '70s has rid them of spurious later accretions and allows us today to enjoy their original beauty.

Zagorsk

'Appearance of the Virgin to St Sergius' (1525). This shroud was a gift from the Muscovite Grand Duke Vasily III and his wife, Solomonia Saburova, and is woven from gold and silver thread, and silk set with pearls and rubies in gold mountings. The inscription is a prayer for the gift of an heir, a theme echoed in the pictures: centre, the appearance of the Virgin to Sergius; at the corners, 'The Annunciation', 'The Nativity of Christ' and 'The Birth of John the Baptist'; and on the lower strip, 'St Anne conceiving (the Virgin)' and 'St Elizabeth conceiving (John the Baptist)'.

Chalice (1597), the gift of Boris Godunov; engraved gold, with niello and precious stones.

The Shroud of Christ, from the workshops of Prince Staritsky (detail). The gift of Prince Vladimir Andreyevich Staritsky and his mother, Princess Yevfrosinia. Silk, with gold and silver threads. A masterpiece of Russian medieval embroidery, like all the products of this celebrated workshop, and noteworthy especially for its dramatic quality and the beauty and exceptional craftsmanship of the needlework. Its subject, the women weeping at the foot of the Cross, is said to have been chosen by the Staritsky family in premonition of their massacre by agents of Ivan the Terrible. The figure of St Sergius was introduced into the scene to act as the family's intercessor.

St Matthew, illumination from a New Testament (1540s). Note the elaborate complexity of the architectural background and the subtle proportions and lavish colour of this little work.

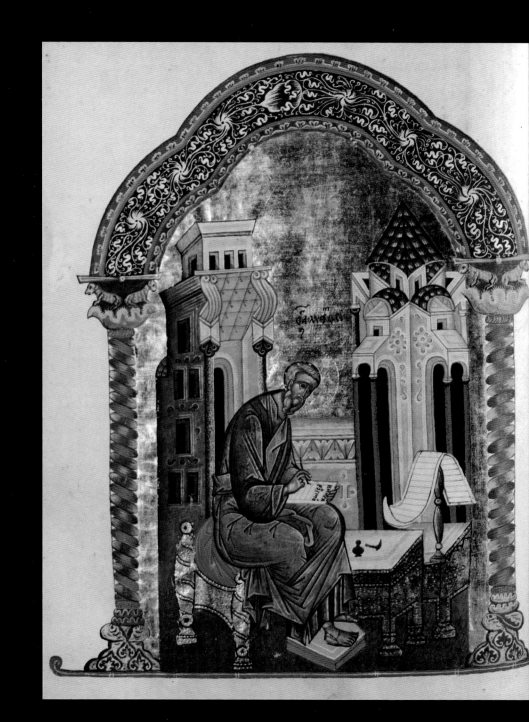

Mitre, gold, with precious stones, silver, pearls, embossed work and enamel, the gift of Princess Anna Mstislavskaya.

Oklad, or cover, of the 'Trinity' icon by Andrei Rublev, detail. Gold and silver, with precious stones and pearls. The gold crowns were a gift from Boris Godunov at the end of the sixteenth century, the Panhagia from his son, Fyodor Godunov, in the early seventeenth century; the hangings were given by Tsar Mikhail, the first of the Romanovs, in 1626.

PERESLAVL

Pereslavl-Zalessky straddles the highly important trade route leading north to Yaroslavl and Archangel. The traveller approaching the city is greeted by superb views of the huge Lake Pleshcheev, on whose southern shore Pereslavl is situated, and of the surrounding hills. The natural beauty of the area is complemented by the city's architectural disposition: the great ensembles of the ancient monasteries dominate the hills, while the serene city centre, with its low wooden and masonry buildings, including some small, elegant eighteenth-century churches, spreads out along the even shores of the lake and the banks of the little River Trubezh which flows into it. The charm of Pereslavl-Zalessky's calm and unhurried provincial life is so seductive that its great monuments to a heroic past – such as the original earth ramparts and the twelfth-century limestone Cathedral of the Transfiguration of the Saviour – take us almost by surprise.

The city's name takes us back to that early period of Russian history so redolent of valour and military glory – Kievan Rus. 'Pereslavl' is derived from two old Russian words: *pereyat* (now *perenyat*), meaning 'to achieve' and *slava*, meaning 'glory'. Many medieval cities bore similar names, including Pereyaslavl Kievsky, where the Trubezh meets the Dnieper; Pereyaslavl Ryazansky (now Ryazan); and Pereslavets Bolgarsky. The northern Pereyaslavl of this chapter acquired the suffix *Zalessky*, which aptly describes its remote position, *za lessami* (literally, 'beyond the forests') of the Oka and Moscow rivers, on the marches of the Rostov and Suzdal territories. The 'ya' of Pereyaslavl was dropped in the fifteenth century.

Between the eighth and tenth centuries this area was populated by Meryan tribes. Gradually, over the following two hundred years, it was colonized by Slav settlers. Their ancient fortress-town of Kreshchin, whose ramparts have survived, was situated on the northeast shore of the lake. When Yuri Dolgoruky became prince of northeastern Rus in the first half of the twelfth century he decided to create a more powerful stronghold. He abandoned Kreshchin and moved to the site of the present Pereslavl, where, according to a contemporary chronicle, he 'built a new town, larger than before, and a stone church dedicated to the [Transfiguration of the] Holy Saviour' (1157). Yuri's ambition was to succeed his father, Vladimir Monomakh, to the throne of Kiev, and his choice of names for the town and its river was a conscious echo of Pereyaslavl Kievsky and the Trubezh that ran through Kiev.

Pereslavl's defensive role was to guard the important trade route that wound via the River Nerl to the Klyazma and Oka rivers, and via Nerl Vodzhskaya to the Volga and Novgorod. In 1175 it became the capital of a principality within the larger state of Suzdalia. In 1194 its ramparts were reinforced with wooden walls and twelve towers. The ramparts were protected to the north and east by the River Trubezh and its tributary, the Murash, and to the southwest by a deep moat.

Pereslavl's earliest major building, the Cathedral of the Transfiguration, displays the artistry worthy of a princely capital. It was the work of architects from Volyn and Galich, in southwestern Russia, who had learned the techniques and practices of builders versed in the Polish Romanesque tradition. Many of these techniques are evident in the Cathedral of the Transfiguration, including the use of blocks of squared and dressed limestone (rather than the more

The Goritsky Monastery, seen from the north. The dark silhouettes are the domes of the Cathedral of the Dormition (1759); in the background is the five-domed Church of All Saints (late seventeenth century). The monastery, high on a hill above the city, dominates Pereslavl.

Detail of the drum and *zakomary* of the Monastery of the Transfiguration of the Saviour (1157). The severity of this building, the oldest in northeast Rus, is modified by the *zakomary*, pilasters, and the stepped triangles on the top of the drum.

Pereslavl

usual brick), the recessed portals and windows, and the application of various decorative elements, such as the horizontal ledge midway up the façades and the elegantly simple friezes: arches running around the apses, zigzags around the drum.

In its basic structure, the cathedral typifies – and in fact was a prototype for – the most characteristic style of church in twelfth-century Suzdalia: cruciform, with *zakomary*, three apses and a single cupola. Many people consider it the finest of these churches, by virtue of the clarity and harmony of its composition and its superb proportions. (The present roof of the dome dates from the sixteenth century; the original followed the shape of the cupola).

The gallery reserved for the prince may be seen in the west end of the cathedral. An opening in the west end of the north wall led from the cathedral to passages giving access to the prince's courtyard.

The cathedral's interior is impressive in the disciplined precision of its massive proportions and the spacious, powerful dynamic of its central drum and cupola. Simple Romanesque capitals mark the springing of the central arches. In the twelfth century the floors were laid with glazed ceramic tiles: the present floor of white stone tiles dates from the sixteenth century.

For many years the Cathedral of the Transfiguration remained the city's only stone building. In the thirteenth century Pereslavl not only suffered the depredations of the Tatar forces under the command of Batu Khan but was twice (in 1281 and 1293) devastated by fire during times of feudal strife. Control of Pereslavl was a factor in the struggle between Muscovy and the principality of Tver for control of Russia. In 1302 the city was united with Moscow. After repelling an attack by Tver in 1304, Pereslavl remained permanently part of the growing Muscovite State and an important trading centre.

Many monasteries were established on the outskirts of the city during the thirteenth and fourteenth centuries. The earliest, the Nikitsky, built on the northern side, was actually founded in the twelfth century by the ascetic Nikita, a zealot and the first local saint. In his youth Nikita was a tax collector, infamous for his exceptional harshness. One day, while reading the Book of Isaiah, he was seized with the spirit of repentance, abandoned his secular life and his family, bound himself with iron fetters and lived out the rest of his life on a pillar in constant prayer and meditation. After his apparently motiveless murder, the monastery was built on the place of his martyrdom.

In 1304 the Fyodorovsky Monastery was founded to the south of the city, in commemoration of the victory over Tver, and the Goritsky Monastery (now the History and Art Museum) was built nearby, a little nearer the city centre. All of these monastery buildings were made of wood. The use of stone in monasteries became common only in the sixteenth century, as a consequence of the patronage and involvement of Muscovy and its rulers.

Daniil, father confessor to Vasily III, Grand Duke of Muscovy, and godfather to Ivan the Terrible, came from the Goritsky Monastery. In 1508 he founded the Trinity Monastery, not far from the Goritsky. Subsequently renamed the Danilov Monastery after him, it was the first in Pereslavl to acquire a stone cathedral, dedicated to the Trinity (1532), designed by Grigory Borisov. It recalls the style of the early sixteenth-century buildings in the Moscow Kremlin, especially in the elegant contours of the cornice, the archivolts of the *zakomary* (here contained within a squared-off façade), the keel-shaped portals and the massive tent roof of the belfry.

These characteristics were repeated in the original Cathedral of St Nikita the Martyr, commissioned by Vasily III for the Nikitsky Monastery. All that survives from this building is the small chapel of Nikita of Pereslavl, a single-domed structure with trefoil motifs on the façades.

The monastery's most important building, dating from the reign of Ivan the Terrible, exemplified the new, more grandiloquent style identified with the Tsar. This was the second Cathedral of St Nikita the Martyr, constructed, together with its surrounding walls and towers, between 1561 and 1564. This imposing five-domed cathedral has two chapels at the east end: the Nikita (surviving from the old cathedral) and the new All Saints Chapel.

The massive walls and towers of the monastery have rows of embrasures at the ground and upper levels, as well as machiolations and large turrets. To this day the monastery, high in the hills overlooking the city, has the appearance of a fortress; in the sixteenth century, certainly, its defensive capability was equal to that of any urban fortifications.

Pereslavl

The Cathedral of the Transfiguration of the Saviour. An outstanding example of twelfth-century Kievan art. The limestone masonry and much of the decorative detail reveal a Romanesque influence, for instance in the horizontal ledge running along the middle of the façades, and the arcades. The arched opening on the second floor of the western section of the north façade was placed at the level of the horizontal ledge indicating the floor of the choir gallery. It was originally a private entrance from the royal quarters to the cathedral.

Pereslavl

The Church of the Metropolitan
Peter. In the early fourteenth
century a court sat in Pereslavl to
judge the case of Peter, who had
been slandered by the
Archbishop of Tver. The original
wooden church built in
commemoration of this event
was replaced by the present
stone building in 1585. In the
nineteenth century a new bell
tower replaced the original tent-
roofed building.

In the next two hundred years a number of other buildings were added to the Nikitsky Monastery; these include the refectory Church of the Annunciation, the residence of the Father Superior and the Church of St Nicholas, a tent-roofed bell tower (1668) and additional accommodation for monks. In 1818 a bell tower replaced the entrance tower and the Church (over the gates) of the Archangel Gabriel.

In 1557, while Ivan the Terrible and his wife, the Tsaritsa Anastasia, were returning to Moscow after a visit to Pereslavl to consecrate a church, the Tsaritsa gave birth to their son, Fyodor. At his birthplace, some 4½ miles south of Pereslavl, the Holy Cross was later built. It was replaced in the seventeenth century by a stone chapel, which has survived (although in its late nineteenth-century restored state). In that same year of 1557 construction began on the Cathedral of St Fyodor Stratilat (commissioned by Ivan himself) in the Fyodorovsky Monastery, founded to commemorate the birth of the Tsarevich. This rather ponderous-looking brick structure originally had high porches on three sides; these were replaced by a gallery in 1704. Other monastery buildings added later include the low wall (1681), the bell tower (1705), the Church of the Feast of the Presentation (1710) and the Kazan Church (1714).

New building in Pereslavl itself – as opposed to the monasteries – was relatively sparse during most of the sixteenth century. The Church of the Metropolitan Peter was erected only in 1585, not far from the Cathedral of the Transfiguration, on the site of the former royal residence. During the early fourteenth century, the Archbishop of Tver had accused Pereslavl's Metropolitan Peter of selling ecclesiastical offices. A wooden church commemorating the trial, in 1313, and complete exoneration of Metropolitan Peter, who was subsequently canonized, had stood on this site since the fourteenth century. The stone church that replaced it is of very unusual design. Raised on a high basement storey and surrounded by a gallery, it is in the form of a Greek cross, with short transepts, each with a façade topped with *zakomary*. A low octagonal drum supports a high tent roof and a small onion dome. The original tent-roofed bell tower was replaced in 1826 by a classically inspired tower.

The many churches built in the sixteenth century required a large number of icons, including those destined for iconostases. Some that have survived are in the collection of the local museum, now housed in the Goritsky Monastery.

Perhaps the most richly endowed of Pereslavl's monasteries in the seventeenth and eighteenth centuries, the Goritsky owned some 5,000 serfs. The scale of its wealth may be inferred by comparing this figure with the population of Pereslavl itself. The city declined sharply as a result of the Time of Troubles and the Polish incursions, when it was half destroyed. By the mid-seventeenth century it had recovered somewhat and had 4,566 inhabitants, but the plague of 1654 claimed nearly three-quarters of the population, which, even as late as 1678, numbered only 1,342.

Construction on the Goritsky Monastery recommenced in the mid-seventeenth century with a new stone retaining wall, with two gates and three corner towers. The wall underwent many repairs and reconstructions, but the Holy Gates, at the southeast corner, approached from the Moscow road, have survived, as have the East Entrance Gates.

The Holy Gates were surrounded by the richly decorated Church of St Nicholas, which was rebuilt in the eighteenth century. Next to the Gates was a small arched pedestrian entrance with a richly ornamented keel shaped portal. The equally remarkable East Entrance Gates are buttressed by two pairs of squat, round columns, above which are decorative recessed stone panels, two of them containing small horses in high relief.

The Danilov Monastery acquired some fine buildings in the late seventeenth century, when Count I. P. Baryatinsky, who had taken the cowl under the name of Father Yefrem, financed construction of the All Saints Church (1687), the refectory and Church of the Adoration of the Virgin (1695), some monks' cells (1696) and a boundary wall (1700). The tent-roofed bell tower was built by masons from Kostroma in 1689. An arched loggia joined the Cathedral of the Trinity to the refectory, which, with its richly ornamented stonework and brickwork, is especially noteworthy. Between 1662 and 1668 the interior walls of the Cathedral of the Trinity were decorated with superb frescoes – the first major work from the famous *artel* of artists led by Guri Nikitin and Sila Savin.

Detail from the surround of the icon 'Nikita Pereslavsky and scenes from his life' (sixteenth century). A detail of the central panel is shown on page 119.

Iconostasis from the village of Spasskoye (sixteenth century). Such iconostases, made up of several vertical boards bearing three rows of icons – showing the deesis, the feast-days and the prophets – were generally to be found in small churches or the side chapels of larger churches and cathedrals. They are excellent examples of the sixteenth-century icon painters' use of line and colour to achieve the most expressive effect.

The youth of Peter the Great, his love of the sea and his interest in shipbuilding, occupy a special chapter in the history of Pereslavl. He first visited the city in 1688 and soon set up a shipyard, which began work on a flotilla; its first vessels were launched on Lake Pleshcheev in 1689. The solemn inauguration of the Russian fleet took place on 1 August 1692, an event marked by celebrations lasting more than a month. The programme included gun salutes from on board ship and ashore, bell ringing and a religious procession from all the city's churches to the lake, as well as military and naval manoeuvres. A Museum of the Fleet of Peter the Great was founded in 1722, but in 1783 a fire destroyed eighty-seven of the ships exhibited there. The sole surviving ship of the first fleet, the *Fortuna*, may still be seen at the Botik Museum, near Pereslavl, along with some triumphal gates, a wooden palace dating from 1852 and a monument to Peter sculpted in the same year.

In the eighteenth century building was concentrated in and around the Goritsky Monastery, including the refectory and Church of All Saints (late seventeenth century, surrounding buildings mid-eighteenth century), the Cathedral of the Dormition (1759) and the bell tower (1760s). The monastery's most illustrious period was between 1744 and 1788, when the archbishops of Pereslavl were resident there. One of them, Amfrosii Zortis-Kamensky, had been Father Superior of the New Jerusalem Monastery, near Moscow, when its Cathedral of the Resurrection – an extraordinary seventeenth-century building consisting mainly of a huge rotunda with a dormer-studded conical roof – was being restored by Bartolomeo Rastrelli. The lavish and ambitious scale of building in Pereslavl at the time was a reflection of his association with this great monastery. The five-domed Cathedral of the Dormition (1757), with its two side chapels, was at the centre of the ensemble. Its great mass is easily visible from the city.

The interior of the Cathedral of the Dormition is of exceptional interest. The light-blue walls and vaults are decorated with very fine rococo white moulded cartouches, garlands and medallions containing paintings. Splendid carved and gilded iconostases adorn the cathedral's sanctuary and side chapels. The design of the cathedral may be attributable to the outstanding Moscow architect Prince Dmitri Ukhtomsky; we know that the interior stucco and moulding are the work of craftsmen from the New Jerusalem Monastery and from Moscow.

The gradual development of craft and trade, together with Pereslavl's increasing prosperity, encouraged the construction, in the late 1700s, of masonry parish churches. Among the best examples are the churches of St Vladimir and St Alexander Nevsky (both 1740s), near the Church of Metropolitan Peter, and the baroque Church of St Simeon Stolpnik (1771).

The well-known River Settlement, situated nearby along the banks of the Trubezh River, has a charm of its own. A fishing settlement has existed here since Neolithic times, and 'Pereslavl herring' was served at the tables of the grand dukes of Muscovy even in the fourteenth century. The settlement has retained much of its picturesque medieval character. Peasant huts stand among gardens and orchards. Willows lean over the water, above little planked footpaths, and boats are moored or beached along the river banks. Between the houses fishing nets are hung up to dry. The Church of the Intercession (1789) rises gracefully over the dwellings at the entrance to the settlement; and where the Trubezh flows into the lake the delicate contours of the Church of the Forty Saints (1775) are drawn against a distant background of greenery and water.

The wooden architecture of seventeenth- and eighteenth-century Pereslavl featured much decorative wood carving. This craft was applied not only to iconostases and religious figures, but also to houses and everyday objects. The carvers brought in to decorate Tsar Peter's ships introduced a fine tradition of sculpture to Pereslavl, and local craftsmen were also greatly influenced in the 1750s by their fellows at work on the interior of the Dormition Cathedral.

The best way to complete a visit to Pereslavl-Zalessky is to make a tour of the ramparts. The lake and the monasteries are clearly visible in the distance, while the city below, its modest churches dominated by the pure, crystal-clear lines of the Cathedral of the Transfiguration, appears almost close enough to touch.

Far right
Little man, painted wood (late seventeenth or early eighteenth century). A good example of popular folk art. The purpose of the figure is uncertain but it probably decorated the gate of some country estate. It is remarkable for its naive realism and the precision of its everyday detail; it has a certain stylized circularity, perhaps intended to preserve a 'memory' of the log from which it was carved.

Right
Nikola Mozhaisky. Wooden painted sculpture (late seventeenth century). Similar statues of Nikola, a sword in his right hand and a model of a church in his left, were widespread in Rus; they were all derived from the statue of the saint in Mozhaisk.

Pereslavl

129

ROSTOV

Rostov is a quiet and peaceful city—except on holidays, when thousands of tourists throng the streets and the air is filled with the sound of its churchbells pealing out over the lake. At such times the atmosphere recalls the period in the city's history, the twelfth century, when it was first dubbed Rostov Veliky—Rostov the Great.

The low, flat shoreline of Lake Nero gives the countryside around Rostov a sense of endless space stretching into the distance. The city skyline, with its profusion of onion domes, tent roofs and spires encircling the kremlin, rises magically over the landscape. To the left of the ensemble (viewed from the lake) the silhouette of the Holy Saviour-Yakovlevsky Monastery offers a comparably rich and imposing vista. In fact, the visitor approaching Rostov along the Moscow road might easily mistake the Yakovlevsky Monastery for the renowned Rostov kremlin itself, so splendid are its buildings.

The actual kremlin, dating from the most illustrious period in the city's history, the late 1600s, is undoubtedly Rostov's main attraction; but if one ignores the surrounding architectural ensembles one gets a somewhat distorted impression of the city, whose history is actually imprinted in all of its many monuments, both early (such as the sixteenth-century Church of the Ascension and the Avraamiev Monastery) and late (such as the Holy Saviour-Yakovlevsky Monastery, whose buildings span the seventeenth to nineteenth centuries).

Rostov is more than a thousand years old; the first mention of it appears in a chronicle written in the year 862. Originally a settlement of the Ugro-Finnish Merya tribe, it was colonized, in the tenth and eleventh centuries, by Slavs, who subsequently intermarried with the local inhabitants. Thus the region became a border territory of Kievan Rus, linked by rivers with Tver, Novgorod and cities in the southern part of the country.

In the eleventh century monks from the Kievo-Pechersky Monastery brought Christianity to the area. The efforts of one such proselytizer, Avraamy, resulted in the foundation of the oldest monastery in Russia, that of the Avraamiev Epiphany, in the early eleventh century. Even earlier a fine Cathedral of the Dormition (991) was constructed of oak; it survived until 1160.

The Suzdal and Rostov cathedrals constituted the most important religious centres of the northeastern part of Rus until the rise of Vladimir in the mid-twelfth century. In 1161-62, following the destruction by fire of the old wooden cathedral, Andrei Bogolyubsky, grand duke of Suzdalia, of which Rostov was then a part, erected the stone Dormition Cathedral. It was rebuilt in 1213-1231 by Prince Konstantin of Rostov, the city's first ruler after it gained independence in 1207. Destroyed by Mongol invaders, the cathedral was rebuilt several times; the present building dates from the sixteenth century. The remaining carved limestone blocks of the thirteenth-century cathedral (displayed in the museum) bespeak a cultural tradition as courtly, extravagant and refined as that of Vladimir.

Rostov was razed to the ground by the Tatars in 1238, and in the following centuries suffered many other depredations as a result of Tatar invasions and feudal wars. At the same time, however, the city became an archiepiscopal centre, with its own tradition of icon painting, which produced outstanding works (many of which are collected in the museum). In 1474

Above

Pectoral cross, *finift* or enamel (nineteenth century).

Left

Rostov kremlin (1670–1690), seen from the lake. A view from the south which perfectly conveys the historical relationship between the central ensemble and the surrounding buildings. The tall white churches seem to glisten in the dusk of the short winter day.

it became part of Muscovy. Contemporary chronicles describe an intensive building programme in the late fifteenth and early sixteenth centuries, of which nothing, unfortunately, has survived.

By the end of the sixteenth century, Rostov's position on the trade route between Moscow and Archangel, on the White Sea, had invested it with a new importance. Already, in 1553, Ivan the Terrible had ordered the Avraamiev Monastery, which controlled the local route and river crossings, to build the Church of the Epiphany in commemoration of his victory the previous year over the Tatars of Kazan. This splendid building was to be the model for many other monuments in seventeenth-century Rostov and neighbouring Yaroslavl. The five-domed cathedral, with façades rising to *zakomary*, is flanked by a single-domed chapel to the northwest, a columnar bell tower to the southwest and a tent-roofed chapel to the southeast. All these buildings stand on a raised, vaulted basement storey and together create an asymmetric but perfectly balanced monumental ensemble.

A few years later Ivan the Terrible dispatched his 'state architect', Andrei Maly, to Rostov to build the Church of the Ascension (1566), which was financed by the Tsar himself and is better known as the Church of Isidor the Blessed, to whom one of the side chapels was dedicated. The façades of this simple church include many features of the Italianate style of kremlin architecture; the design is completed by a crossed arch, whose lines repeat the triple-fan lines of the façades, and a windowed onion dome.

The gradual increase in Rostov's importance was interrupted by the devastation of the Polish and Swedish invasions in the early 1600s. A census of 1619 describes the majority of the city's properties as either destroyed by fire or in an impoverished condition. Not surprisingly, one of the priorities, as the Time of Troubles drew to a close, was the construction of new fortifications. Completed in 1633, these consisted of two earth ramparts with moats. The work was carried out under the supervision of a Dutchman, Jan Cornelius Rodenburg. Parts of these ramparts still survive.

In the mid-seventeenth century the appearance of Rostov was dramatically transformed with the construction of its kremlin. This kremlin differs from those in many other cities, which were built in medieval times and which served from the outset as fortresses. It was built by Rostov's Metropolitan Iona Sisoyevich, who had nurtured hopes of becoming Patriarch of Russia, after the reform-minded Patriarch Nikon had fallen into disfavour with the Tsar. Soon after his candidacy was rejected, in 1664, Iona returned to Rostov and embarked on the splendid ecclesiastical city-within-a-city that later (in the early nineteenth century) became known as the kremlin.

For thirty years, from 1670, the centre of Rostov was one vast building site, where teams of builders and artists worked ceaselessly on the Metropolitan's Palace, various civic buildings and churches and, of course, the walls and towers encircling the whole complex.

Previous spread
Rostov kremlin, general view from the southwest. From left to right: the corner-tower, the five-domed Church of St John the Divine (1683), the five-domed Church of Grigory the Divine (seventeenth century); centre, the circular Sadovaya Tower, beyond it, the onion domes of the Cathedral of the Dormition (second half of sixteenth century), the Church of the Resurrection (seventeenth century), and, tallest of all, the Church of the Saviour on the
Square (1675), set on its high ground floor (*podklet*), with the square tower of the Derevyanniye (Wooden) Gate in front of it; right, a circular corner tower, and, behind the walls, houses and other secular buildings.

Right
View of the west wall of the Rostov kremlin. Between the corner towers is the main entrance to the kremlin and, above it, the Church of St John the Divine. To the right of the corner tower is the low wall of the former Grigorievsky Monastery, which was closed in the sixteenth century and became the metropolitan's garden in the seventeenth. St Sergius Radonezhsky, founder of the Trinity-St Sergius Monastery, was a monk here.

Although the Rostov kremlin is surrounded by a high stone wall and towers, it does not have the density of most Russian citadels. (In fact, it was not called the kremlin until the early nineteenth century.) Towers – nine round and two square – interrupt the perimeter wall at regular intervals, while in the middle of the north and west walls two five-domed churches have been built over the gates, forming beautifully silhouetted groups. All the buildings within the residence are on one raised level, with the formal quarters situated on the upper floor near the elegantly simple Church of the Saviour on the Square (1675), which was intended primarily for the use of the archiepiscopal household.

It seems likely that the architects and those who commissioned them were particularly concerned to create an ensemble in which all the buildings should be visible from the lake. The buildings decrease in size in proportion to their proximity to it. The increase in height and overall size of the buildings in the north section of the ensemble actually culminates outside the walls, to the north of the kremlin, in the magnificent five-domed Cathedral of the Dormition. No single one of these buildings obscures any other, and the highest and largest – the cathedral – is the farthest away. The free and unencumbered positioning of the various components of the scene is nicely combined with the low houses and with two churches adjoining the kremlin itself; Our Saviour in the Market (1690) and the Nativity of the Virgin (late seventeenth century).

The date of the existing Cathedral of the Dormition cannot, unfortunately, be ascertained from any contemporary sources, but it was probably completed sometime in the sixteenth century, and is clearly inspired by the great fifteenth- and sixteenth-century cathedrals, such as the Dormition Cathedrals of the Moscow Kremlin and of Zagorsk. The simple façades articulated with pilasters and blind arcades, the slit windows and the massive proportions of the drums and cupolas are among their distinctive shared features. The regularity of form in these buildings bespeaks their role in symbolizing the authority of the state. Some of the features peculiar to the Rostov cathedral are the more elongated onion domes, covered with overlapping tiles, the relatively slender and richly decorated drums, and the keel-shaped *zakomary*. A porch with an arcade punctuated with pendant shapes, called *girki*, adjoins the cathedral on the south side.

One of the city's most famous attractions is the bell tower (1687) located between the cathedral and the kremlin. Not, in fact, tower-shaped, it is a rectangular structure crowned by four onion domes. The taller end was designed to accommodate the largest of the thirteen immense bells, called 'Sysoi', which was cast in 1689 and weighs 32 tonnes. The sound of the Rostov bells was first heard again in the 1960s after many years of silence.

Rostov kremlin, view from the southeast. Left, the dark, low wall of the former Grigorievsky Monastery; behind it, part of the tower over the Derevyanniye Gate; centre, the southeast corner tower, with the upper part of the Church of the Saviour on the Square seen beyond it.

Because they were built to guard the metropolitan's palace, rather than for military purposes, the walls and towers of the Rostov kremlin have a somewhat festive air. Even the overhanging parapets contribute to the upward surge of the masonry, a movement continued by the outlines of the cube-like turrets atop the towers, by the two domed churches built above the gates, and, finally, by the small belfried watchtowers set along the walls. The towers sport rows of elaborately framed windows which admit light to the intriguing circular rooms set at the level of the passages built into the walls.

The two gates, one set in the north, the other in the west wall of the kremlin, for pedestrian and equestrian traffic respectively, are flanked by large round towers and surmounted by churches: the Church of the Resurrection (1670) on the north gate and that of St John the Divine (1683) on the west. Together with the adjacent towers, and the belfried watchtowers on the walls, they create a lively interplay of slopes and rhythms.

The two five-domed churches are particularly elegant examples of seventeenth-century architecture. The façades of the Resurrection Church are studded with inset square panels containing decorative motifs, above which are diamond-paned windows with arched baroque surrounds. Inside, the church is richly decorated with frescoes. The Church of St John the Divine has an exceptionally graceful shape with a strong vertical emphasis. The central mass of the building rises to *zakomary* with shallow, straight-angled roofs. The interior west walls of both churches include niches which once contained empty jars – a device used to improve the acoustics and thus enhance the beautiful choral singing which is an integral part of Russian Orthodox services.

All the buildings within the kremlin are grouped around a courtyard. The Resurrection and Hodegetria churches (the latter built in 1698) are situated to the north; the main building of the metropolitan's palace, known as the Samuilov building, together with the *Krasnaya Palata* or Red Palace (1680), for important guests, stand on the south; while the west of the square is bounded by the gate church of St John the Divine. The Samuilov building was radically reconstructed in the eighteenth and nineteenth centuries; nowadays, partly restored, it houses the Museum of History and Art. The courtyard contains a small pond whose tranquil waters mirror the surrounding buildings. Living quarters for the metropolitan's household line the east and south walls of the kremlin, their roofs still bearing rows of high chimneys topped with decorative chimneypots whose silhouettes add a homely and human element to the ensemble.

The most architecturally interesting parts of the inner nucleus of the kremlin are the formal rooms of the metropolitan's palace – the spacious White (refectory) Chamber, the 'Preceding' Chamber (used for audiences with the metropolitan) – and the adjoining Church of the Saviour on the Square, all of them on a raised storey.

Rostov kremlin, view from the tower of the Water Gate. Centre, the Church of the Saviour on the Square with its two-tiered dome; between it and the Samuilov building on the right is a small open area, known as Seni Square. In the distance are the five domes of Grigory the Divine; left, along the wall towards the corner tower and then along the east wall, are the well-preserved apartments and servants' quarters of the metropolitan's palace. In the distance is Lake Nero.

Rostov kremlin. View along the wall from the corner of the northwest tower to the Church of the Resurrection of Christ.

Gallery of the Church of the Resurrection Over the Gate of the Rostov kremlin. It surrounds the church on three sides, with a staircase down to ground level at one corner. Light pours through regularly-spaced windows with figures of saints frescoed in the apertures. The frescoes date from about 1675.

Rostov

The Church of the Resurrection. General views of the interior showing details of the original frescoes. This is one of the most unusual interiors in medieval Russian architecture. The side walls of the rectangular building are divided into three parts by pairs of half-columns on high bases. The frescoes were painted in about 1675. The east section has three features peculiar to Rostov churches; a high *solea* (a raised floor in front of the altar) with a painted parapet, an arcade on powerful columns with three apertures, forming a type of base for the iconostasis, and the iconostasis itself, painted in fresco on the east wall and crowned with a colossal crucifixion scene.

Rostov

The Rostov kremlin. View along the south wall to the Church of the Saviour on the Square. In front of the church one can see the arches and windows of the White Chamber of the metropolitan's palace.

South porch of the Cathedral of the Dormition, on the main square between the Cathedral itself and the north wall of the kremlin; in the background one can see the lower tiers of the bell tower. The arcade, with hanging pendants, or *girki*, a very popular feature in the seventeenth century, is a conscious reference to the west porch of the Cathedral of the Dormition in Moscow. The small columns and bases have a faceted finish typical of their period.

The austerely elegant Church of the Saviour on the Square (1675), although relatively small, is the main vertical element of this group. Looking from the direction of the lake, one can see the church rising gracefully above the kremlin walls and towers, its four-gabled roof and façades recalling the nearby (and earlier) Church of St Isidor. The dome rests on a drum whose base is surrounded by a row of zigzags and which in turn rests on a square, windowed base.

All of the kremlin buildings and walls are interconnected by a series of raised, arched walkways. It is thus possible to walk around the entire complex on its upper level, enjoying the views of the palace and the neighbouring arched galleries. An equally varied panorama is visible from the passages and promenades, and especially from the watchtower lookouts.

The Saviour-Yakovlevsky Monastery is Rostov's second most important architectural ensemble. Three large five-domed churches and a wall, with six towers and bell towers, adjacent to the Church of the Saviour on the Sands (late 1600s) create a group of silhouettes as beautiful as those of the kremlin. In fact, two monasteries stand side by side here: the Holy Saviour (founded in the thirteenth century) was absorbed in the late eighteenth century by its neighbour, the Yakovlevsky (founded in the fourteenth century).

The five-domed Cathedral of the Immaculate Conception (originally dedicated to the Trinity) was built by Metropolitan Iona in 1686 and is the oldest of the Yakovlevsky Monastery buildings. Both it and the Church of the Saviour make use of the same compositional techniques to be found in the kremlin buildings, although the monastery is dominated by the classical forms favoured in the late eighteenth and early nineteenth centuries. The monastery wall, also completed in 1786, incorporates towers and a bell tower over the gates, as well as cells for the monks, priors and father superior.

North of the Cathedral of the Immaculate Conception is the Church of St Dmitri, commissioned from the Moscow architect Nazarov by Count Sheremetov (to commemorate the birth of his son Dmitri) and built by his serf architects Mironov and Dushkin between 1774 and 1801. The façades of this splendid classical five-domed edifice are graced by monumental porticoes decorated with sculptures and bas reliefs. Between 1824 and 1836 the similarly five-domed Yakovlevsky Church was built onto the north side of the cathedral, with all the elements of its classical design being consciously modelled on the neighbouring St Dmitri.

Towards the end of the eighteenth century the pace of life in Rostov slackened considerably. The city became part of a newly established province whose administrative centre was located in Yaroslavl, to which the metropolitan's headquarters were transferred. The architectural centre of Rostov gradually fell into decline. A systematic general plan, imposed on the outer residential parts of the city at this time, left the centre unaffected. Rostov was never again to experience the intense architectural and artistic creativity of its heyday.

Left, the Cathedral of the Dormition and, in the centre, the bell tower or belfry (1687), celebrated not only as a work of architecture but also for the glorious sound of its bells; right, the north section of the kremlin wall, with its towers, and the Church of the Resurrection Over the Gates.

147

Left

The Church of the Ascension (sixteenth century). Commissioned by Ivan the Terrible and built by his court architect, Andrei Maly, this is similar to many elegant and ornate churches built at the same period on private estates. The interior frescoes date from the 1720s.

Right

The Epiphany Church of the Avraamiev Monastery (1553). Founded in commemoration of the capture of Kazan, it is Rostov's earliest surviving stone building. The main five-domed structure, three side chapels, tent-roofed bell tower, gallery and west vestibule, all on a single, slightly raised foundation, form a complex composition reminiscent of St Basil's Cathedral on Red Square in Moscow, which was built at about the same time. The original roof was replaced in the first half of the eighteenth century, as was the roof of the southeast chapel. The great frescoes in the church itself date from the mid-eighteenth century.

Rostov

Artistic life was, however, stimulated to some extent by the development of the art of *finift*, or enamelwork. *Finift* was used to decorate church plate, liturgical books, and the settings, frames and covers of icons; in addition, small icons were themselves produced by this technique, which probably originated in the mid-eighteenth century. Until the mid-nineteenth century the enamellers, who had formed their own guild in 1788, restricted themselves to religious themes; later they adapted their art to the decoration of everyday household objects. (A favourite theme was the view of Rostov from the lake.) Today the tradition continues to thrive and to enjoy a high reputation at home and abroad.

Rostov's special historical and artistic significance was recognized in the nineteenth century, when various initiatives were launched to save and restore the dilapidated buildings of the kremlin. It is thanks largely to these efforts that the kremlin buildings have survived to our day. The interiors of Rostov's churches, all preserved in their original state, are outstanding examples of sacred architecture and contain several series of late seventeenth- and eighteenth-century frescoes, together with magnificent iconostases.

Rostov's archictectural treasures have been carefully restored in recent decades. Ironically enough, a natural disaster gave added urgency to this work when a violent windstorm in 1953 destroyed the upper sections of many buildings, ripping off roofs and toppling onion domes. The subsequent restoration programme became a priority of both government and public. Recent work on the kremlin's western flank has led to the discovery of large stables, which are now being studied and restored.

A visit to Rostov would be incomplete without a side trip to another outstanding monument, situated about two miles from the city along the Moscow road, in the village of Bogoslov. From early times a ferry, operated by the Avraamiev Monastery, has plied across the River Ishna to this tranquil spot. Here one finds the wooden Church of St John the Divine, built in 1689. Its structure is of the long 'ship' type, characteristic of the seventeenth century, consisting of a main sanctuary (here crowned with two superimposed octagons) and a refectory to the west, leading to a bell tower (in this case added later). An overhanging gallery runs around three sides of the whole building (the gallery's fourth, south side collapsed in the nineteenth century). Somewhat later a tent-roofed bell tower with a traceried belfry was added to the west side of the church. Inside, the original *tyablovy* iconostasis (that is, an iconostasis made of solid timbers with icons painted directly on them), with icons dating from the sixteenth to the eighteenth century, has been preserved, together with the original portals, doors and benches lining the walls.

The Church of St Dmitri (1801). This masterpiece was commissioned on the birth of his son by Count Sheremetov from the celebrated Moscow architect Nazarov. Niches in the façades contain statues, and multi-figured bas reliefs run along the upper walls of the refectory. The lower tiers of the bell tower may just be seen at the edge of the picture.

YAROSLAVL

Above

General view of the Monastery of the Transfiguration of the Saviour with, behind, the central area of Yaroslavl and the Church of St Michael the Archangel (1682). The monastery, on the bank of the Kotorisl River, predates the period of Mongol domination. Even in its earliest days it was an important centre of culture and had its own seminary. The monastery's principal buildings – the cathedral, bell tower and refectory – date from the sixteenth century; the stone walls and the Holy Gate were rebuilt in the seventeenth century.

Left

One of the square recesses *(shirinki)* of the porch and gallery of the Church of St John the Baptist in Tolchkovo (1687). The *shirinki* are decorated with polychrome tiles, rather than with the carved rosettes customary in earlier buildings.

Although this Volga city, bearing the name of a grand duke of Kievan Rus, Yaroslav the Wise (1019-54), will shortly be celebrating its millennium, it was obliged to wait hundreds of years for its golden age.

Yaroslavl exemplifies the extraordinary blossoming of Russian culture which occurred in the seventeenth century. The city's art, although imbued with all the sophistication and excellence Moscow could offer, always retained its own local character, and produced works whose scale and ambition sometimes exceeded those of Moscow itself. The seventeenth century, which gave Yaroslavl its magnificent churches, marvellous frescoes and huge carved iconostases, was followed by a more secular era as a provincial centre, when a classical urban environment, of squares, boulevards and pleasant streets, was created around these great works of sacred architecture. Today it is a busy industrial town, producing, among other things, tyres and diesel engines; but the old and new coexist happily in Yaroslavl's riverside setting in the green Kotorisl Valley.

As early as the tenth century, a small Ugro-Finnish settlement existed on the high promontory between the Volga and Kotorisl rivers. Its name was Medvezhy Ugol, or Bear's Corner. In 1010, Yaroslav, then still Grand Duke of Novgorod, was attacked there by a bear which the inhabitants had released from its cage to drive him away. He killed the bear with his axe and later commanded a fortress to be built on the spot. The bear was immortalized in Yaroslavl's coat of arms, where it appears to this day.

Yaroslavl then became a border fortification of the Rostov principality and remained a small town until the mid-twelfth century. The rise of the principality of Suzdalia in the second half of the twelfth century gave a new importance to the region and to Yaroslavl itself.

In 1218 Yaroslavl became a capital, and construction in stone was begun. As early as 1215 the foundations of the Cathedral of the Dormition (no longer extant) had been laid by Konstantin, son of Vsevolod. In the course of the century the fortress built on the promontory, known locally as the Strelka, became the architectural centre of the city. Two monasteries were founded outside the city – the Petrovsky on the Volga and the Transfiguration of Our Saviour on the Kotorisl, and the stone Transfiguration Cathedral was built, together with its attached Church of the Entry into Jerusalem (1224). By 1222 the city could boast seventeen churches, most of them built of brick with limestone ornamentation. The main influence discernible in this architecture is that of the city of Vladimir, whose refined style affected other works, such as the exquisite Transfiguration Testament and the icon known as 'Christ with the Golden Hair' from the Dormition Cathedral. Both of these examples of fine early thirteenth-century Byzantine-style art are distinguished by the subtlety of their treatment of colour and rhythm, complex and somewhat mannered in the miniatures but tranquil and contemplative in the icon.

Life changed dramatically in 1238, after the area was ravaged by Tatar forces under Batu Khan, who put down all resistance with great cruelty. One of the bloodiest battles took place in 1257 outside the walls of Yaroslavl on the bank of the Kotorisl, on a hill which to this day bears the name Tugovaya (from *tuga* meaning 'grief').

In the fourteenth and fifteenth centuries Yaroslavl remained a small principality which gradually came under the dominance of the rulers of Moscow. At this time Russian art was dramatic and tragic in character – a mood reflected in an outstanding fourteenth-century Yaroslavl icon, 'The Tolgskaya Virgin' (1314). The court kept alive, to some extent, the tradi-

The Cathedral of the
Transfiguration of Our Saviour
(1516) seen from the northwest.
Originally the cathedral, the
design of which was strongly
influenced by the Italian-
inspired architecture of the
Moscow Kremlin, had an open,
arched, two-tiered gallery on
three of its sides. In the
seventeenth century the open
gallery along the east façade
was replaced by a closed version
intended to house the
monastery library. The library
contained the original
manuscript of the celebrated
epic, 'The Lay of the Host of Igor'
until 1792, when it was acquired
by Count Musin-Pushkin, only to
be destroyed by fire in Moscow
in 1812.

'Sabaoth', detail of fresco in the
entrance to the Cathedral of the
Transfiguration of the Saviour
(1564).

Yaroslavl

tion of rich and sumptuous art which had flourished before the Mongol invasions, of which a good example is the Fyodorovskoye Testament, commissioned by Prokhor, Metropolitan of Rostov, in memory of Fyodor Stratilat, Duke of Yaroslavl (1240-99). The miniature of Fyodor in majestic pose glorifies his military prowess; another miniature depicts the Apostle John with Metropolitan Prokhor in a highly stylized version of the interior of the Transfiguration of the Saviour Church of the monastery of that name. In this miniature the figure of the Archbishop himself is specially emphasized, presumably at his own request.

The muted colouring of the fifteenth-century icon of the Prophet Elijah (from the Elijah Church) gives it a somewhat provincial character, but its subtly conveyed sense of devotion puts it among the finest works of Muscovite art.

At the end of the fifteenth century the principality of Yaroslavl lost its independence and became part of Muscovy. As a result, the early sixteenth century saw an intensive building programme under the supervision of Moscow architects. The Dormition Cathedral, completely rebuilt between 1501 and 1504, was modelled on its namesake in the Moscow Kremlin and remained, until its destruction in the 1930s, the architectural centre of the Strelka and of Yaroslavl as a whole. The Strelka fortress was surrounded by an earth rampart and wooden walls, behind which arose the commercial quarter and the monasteries.

The Cathedral of the Transfiguration of Our Saviour, constructed in the Transfiguration Monastery between 1505 and 1516, is the oldest building remaining in Yaroslavl today. It strongly reflects the influence of the Italian architects brought in to superintend work on the Moscow Kremlin. The overall form, a three-domed cathedral with *zakomary*, is traditional enough (although less common than one or five domes); what is new is the inviting aspect of the façades. Their grandeur is softened by the cornice at the base of the *zakomary*, set with round windows, and by the arched open gallery running along the western side; originally this encircled the building. The north side of the gallery was replaced in the seventeenth century by a large enclosed porch; later the monastery library was housed here. It was in this library that the only known manuscript copy of the epic 'The Lay of the Host of Igor' was found. In the sixteenth century a refectory, bell tower and stone walls were added to the monastery.

Muscovite traditions are also discernible in Yaroslavl painting, especially in the superb fifteenth-century icons of the Transfiguration Monastery – for example, the Deesis row (containing Christ, the Virgin and important saints), the 'Transfiguration' and the 'Annunciation with the Acathistus (list of prayers) of the Virgin'. The special appeal of these icons lies in the nobility and profound spirituality of the characters, the exquisite artistry with which they are depicted, the beauty of the architectural and landscape motifs, the delicacy of linear rhythm and the subtlety of the colours – all the qualities, indeed, that are associated with the school of Dionysus, the renowned Muscovite painter of the fifteenth century. The monastery's frescoes, painted by Moscow artists in 1563–64, remain one of the finest large-scale cycles dating from the reign of Ivan the Terrible.

The third quarter of the sixteenth century brought new prosperity to the city, especially with the founding of Archangel (in 1584) on the White Sea, through which trade with Western Europe now passed. Located on this trade route, Yaroslavl was transformed from a town on the periphery of Russia into an international trading centre bustling with colonies of English, Dutch and German merchants.

The Church of Elijah the Prophet (1650). Originally the roof ran along the line of the *zakomary* and the arched gallery was open; in the eighteenth and nineteenth centuries the south chapel was remodelled and the north chapel restored. The Rizpolozhensky Chapel at the southwest corner has one of the last tent roofs to be built before they were forbidden by Patriarch Nikon in 1652. The Church of Elijah was commissioned by the Skripin family of merchants. After the destruction of the Cathedral of the Dormition in the 1930s, it became the city's dominant architectural feature.

Yaroslavl

Two views of the interior of the Church of Elijah, remarkable for the excellent condition of its original decoration. Fortunately, the magnificent frescoes of the main church (1680) have never undergone restoration. The frescoes in the chapels and gallery date from the late seventeenth and early eighteenth century. Icons painted in the 1670s and 1680s are preserved in the baroque iconostasis. An immense tent-roofed wooden canopy (1657) is suspended above the altar.

Icon, 'The Ascension of Christ' (second half of the seventeenth century). The boom in church-building in Yaroslavl at this time was accompanied by the production of thousands of magnificent icons, most destined for the new church iconostases. Many have remained in the churches; others may be seen in the Yaroslavl Museum of Art.

Yaroslavl

Right

Detail from a window surround built into the gallery of the Church of St John Chrysostom in Korovniki (1654).

Above, centre

The Church of St John Chrysostom in Korovniki, seen from the west. The photograph shows the wall extending towards the neighbouring winter Church of Our Lady of Vladimir and its Holy Gate (1680); in the background one can see the River Volga.

Below, centre

The Church of Our Lady of Vladimir in Korovniki (1669) and bell tower (1680s). This ensemble of two churches, bell tower, wall and Holy Gate is probably the most beautiful in Yaroslavl. Its situation on the bank of the Volga, near the point where the river is joined by the Kotorisl River, and opposite the kremlin and the Cathedral of the Dormition, is particularly imposing.

Far right

Detail of column in the arched gallery of the Church of St John Chrysostom in Korovniki.

Window of the central apse of the Church of St John Chrysostom in Korovniki and detail. Notable for its beauty, brilliance and size (some 16 feet high), the tiled window surround dates from the late seventeenth century, almost fifty years after the completion of the church, when the manufacture and use of glazed tiles spread from Moscow and changed the appearance of many churches in Yaroslavl. The decoration of St John Chrysostom is particularly lavish.

Yaroslavl

The city's booming economy was brought to a temporary halt in the early 1600s by the Time of Troubles and the Swedish and Polish invasions, but these very events paradoxically helped increase the city's prestige. In 1612 Yaroslavl became the virtual capital of Russia for a year and a half: it was in this once-remote outpost that a national popular army (*opolcheniye*) gathered to defeat the Poles and a government – known as the Council of all Russian Territories – was formed.

After the rout of the Poles and the re-establishment of a truly Russian state, the city of Yaroslavl entered its golden age. Many traders were granted the honoured status and privileges of 'state merchants'. Commerce and crafts, the new wealth-creators, enthusiastically encouraged local culture to blossom, while the patronage of Moscow ensured the participation of the capital's experts in the reconstruction and redecoration of the city (in partnership with Yaroslavl's own artistic traditions).

Work began in 1617 on the Monastery of the Transfiguration of Our Saviour; the walls were rebuilt and a side chapel was added to the Church of the Entry into Jerusalem. Many new stone churches were built between the middle of the seventeenth century and the early years of the eighteenth. These were commissioned by rich merchants and craft guilds, who wanted their buildings to be on a grand scale, but bright and colourful as well. The new churches significantly altered the panorama and skyline of Yaroslavl, especially as they were sited, not on the Strelka promontory, but in the commercial area and in other settlements surrounding the city.

The first of these churches were built to the north of the Strelka, on the bank of the Volga. The earliest is the Church of St Nicholas the Helpful (1621), or St Nicholas Nadein, after a state merchant, Nadea Sveteshnikov, who built it, and modelled on the Transfiguration Monastery cathedral. The church, standing on a raised basement storey, is girdled by two-storeyed galleries; the northern gallery becomes a closed porch. A bell tower was built at the northwest corner and later crowned with a tent roof. The church was crowned by five domes (the corner domes have not survived). Many of the decorative features are derived from Moscow architecture, but the complexity and asymmetry of the composition as a whole, with its clear and powerful architectural volumes, testifies to a distinct Yaroslavl tradition. The church's ornate baroque iconostasis is believed to have been based on a sketch by Fyodor Volkhov, founder of the Russian National Theatre.

The Nazariev merchant family commissioned a group of buildings which included the five-domed Church of the Nativity of Christ, together with a marvellous tent-roofed bell tower over the gates (1644). The most important single building of this period, however, was the Church of Elijah the Prophet (1650), commissioned by the Skripin family of merchants. Although restricting themselves to established architectural techniques the designers of this church gave it a particularly complex and monumental appearance. The two-storey, originally open gallery links five separate asymmetrically disposed elements: the splendid five-domed body of the church itself; the single-domed side chapels on the east end, decorated with beautiful tracery and rows of *kokoshniki*; the bell tower and Rizpolozhensky side chapel, each crowned with an elegant tent roof, on the west end; and finally, the high west porch, with its double-arched portal. The building is a tectonic *tour de force* with its multiplicity of individual, daringly counterpoised volumes.

The walls of the main building are smooth, but the archivolts of the *zakomary* and galleries are relieved by deep panels with carved decorative insertions. The church was stuccoed, with all the decorative detail painted in various colours.

Yaroslavl

The Church of St John the Baptist in Tolchkovo (1687), detail of the domes. Seen from the east, the church appears as a single huge building crowned by fifteen domes – five on the main church and five on each of the two side chapels. Three high porches, a slender bell tower, a wall and a gate complete this elegant architectural ensemble. The cathedral walls are densely covered with reliefs and colourful ornament – *shirinki*, bands of decoration, floral paintings and tiles.

In the seventeenth century, this remarkable church stood on land owned by the Skripin family, but by the end of the eighteenth century the area had been transformed into the main public square. This more or less private church easily adapted itself to the role of city landmark; nowadays, after the destruction of the Strelka ensemble, it is the dominant single element in the urban landscape.

The beauty and architectural perfection of the church is such that it might have seemed a definitive and unimprovable model for the future. Nevertheless, at about this time the architects building the Church of St John Chrysostom (1654) in the Korovniki quarter, across the Kotorisl from the Strelka, departed from this model in two significant ways. They dispensed with a raised basement storey; and they created a strictly symmetrical composition, which consisted of the main, five-domed church, two eastern side chapels with tent roofs, galleries and three high porches sharply projecting from the middle of their façades. The clarity of the structure is complemented by the picturesque charm of the many decorative features, such as clusters of columns at the corners and elaborate window frames.

The formation of the complex continued with the construction of the winter Church of Our Lady of Vladimir (1669). In the 1680s a graceful bell tower with a tent roof was built between the two churches; and in the 1690s a stone wall was constructed which joined the churches' eastern façades with the beautiful perpendicular of the Holy Gates, to form one of the outstanding ensembles of Russian architecture.

Most subsequent church building in Yaroslavl was modelled on St John Chrysostom. Three similar churches were built in the Kotorisl Valley – namely Our Saviour in the Town (1672), St Michael the Archangel (1682) and St Nicholas on the Waters (1672). The most impressive and innovative version was the Church of St John the Baptist in Tolchkovo (1687), in which the small eastern chapels were raised to the height of the large central building, so that the huge eastern façade appeared to be crowned by fifteen domes – the mighty group of five domes of the church itself and the two smaller groups, also of five each, of the side chapels, all covered with overlapping green tiles. A wide porch with projecting smaller porches surrounds the cathedral, whose walls were decorated with attached columns visually linked with rows of tiles, painted in various colours to create a faceted effect.

The Moscow, or Naryshkin baroque style of architecture, which reached Yaroslavl at the end of the seventeenth century, is reflected in the bell tower of St John the Baptist in Tolchkovo and in several churches. One of these, St Nicholas Rublenny (1695), is outstanding for its rational simplicity and the perfection of its composition and silhouette. The brick Church of the Epiphany (1693), combining Muscovite and local traditions, provides a perfect example of high Yaroslavl art. It follows the Moscow model in its rows of *kokoshniki* and five windowless domes, and is girdled by a wide enclosed gallery with porches set into it. A tent-roofed bell tower is situated at the northwest corner. The church is richly decorated with multicoloured tiles running in a belt along the tops of the apses, gallery, porches and *kokoshniki*, and in vertical lines along the walls and cupolas.

Yaroslavl

Gallery of the Church of St John the Baptist in Tolchkovo, the most spacious and richly decorated in Yaroslavl. Note the graceful benches set along the walls, supported by rows of small balusters. The murals date from 1700.

'The Saints of the Orthodox Church' (1695), section from the frescoes in the Church of St John the Baptist in Tolchkovo. This cycle of frescoes is one of the most impressive in the Orthodox world. As well as the canonical series, it contains scenes from the life of John the Baptist; on the west wall are six compositions based on the Song of Songs; and the galleries are painted with biblical scenes. The unique series of paintings on the side walls depicts the complete company of Orthodox saints.

This extraordinary decorative richness, typical of late seventeenth-century Yaroslavl architecture, is due to the tile-manufacturing industry which flourished in Moscow at that time. In Yaroslavl, some churches already built were redecorated with tiles; an example is St John Chrysostom, which is particularly famous for the elaborate frame of its altar window. Other masterpieces of ceramic decoration are the annexes built in the 1690s onto the Church of St Nicholas on the Waters and its adjacent winter Tikhvinskaya Church.

The interiors of Yaroslavl's churches are superb works of art. Their walls are covered with many colourful frescoes; their high iconostases glisten with gilded carving and with the brilliant colours of the icons. Frescoes were executed by the finest artists of the time, often commissioned by the Tsar himself. Teams of painters from Moscow, Kostroma and other cities created the vast cycles which adorned more than thirty churches in the second half of the century alone. The earliest surviving mural, preserved in the Church of St Nicholas Nadein (1640), combines sixteenth-century classical traditions with a new desire to make the narrative element more entertaining and vivid to ordinary people. Later this tendency was augmented by elements of realism which, paradoxically, gave the frescoes some of the qualities of a fairy tale. Painters used their observations of nature and copied Western European models to produce strikingly lifelike poses, situations and facial expressions, and combined them with a symbolic idiom of their own. The finest such murals, in the Church of Elijah the Prophet, are remarkable for their lively rhythm, flowing line and glowing combination of light blue, gold, white and green.

The great traditions of seventeenth-century art remained alive throughout the eighteenth century, but standards gradually declined and new artistic trends made their appearance. The foundation of St Petersburg greatly diminished the importance of the nothern trade route to Europe, via Archangel, and thus Yaroslavl gradually lost its significance.

The first half of the eighteenth century brought the construction of the Church of Saints Peter and Paul (1736), strongly reminiscent of St Petersburg baroque architecture, and the late eighteenth and the early nineteenth centuries saw much residential and domestic construction together with classical city planning, including new ensembles, squares and streets. The principal glories of the city, however, remain its sixteenth- and seventeenth-century churches.

Nowadays many of the most precious objects from these churches are displayed in the Yaroslavl Museum of Art, which is particularly famous for its seventeenth-century icons.

The Church of St Nicholas Rublenny (literally, St Nicholas of the Log Town, 1695), which owes its name to its original position close to the wall of a wooden fortress. There is a harmonious relationship between the plain façades, relieved by large windows at regular intervals, the delicate contours of the five onion domes, and the tent roof of the bell tower. The Church of Our Saviour in the Town can be seen in the background.

The Church of the Epiphany (1693) commissioned by Zubchaninov, a Yaroslavl merchant. Its design, including the two rows of *zakomary* and the array of five windowless domes, shows the influence of the Moscow style. The columnless interior with its high dome is very impressive, but the church's most striking feature is its rich exterior tiling, which is applied in both vertical and horizontal bands, and in the *shirinki*, or square recessed panels, an example of which is seen on the right.

Yaroslavl

KOSTROMA

One of the oldest and most beautiful of medieval Russian cities, Kostroma is also one of the most stylish ensembles produced by late eighteenth- and early nineteenth-century Russian classicism.

Kostroma's distinctive charm springs from this combination of elegant classicism – a splendid classical square standing at the centre of a fan-shaped city plan – and a magnificent skyline created by its medieval monasteries, cathedrals and parish churches. The town is situated on the Volga. Like all of Russia's medieval cities, Kostroma lacked an elegant embankment – riverside areas were used for trade and other utilitarian purposes – but it did offer an impressive panorama, which was both dominated and unified by the two cathedrals standing on a high ridge not far from the river. The Dormition and the Trinity cathedrals rise from the centre of the composition, with the Ipatiev Monastery (with its own cathedral, dedicated to the Trinity) on the left, beyond the point where the little Kostroma River flows into the Volga, and the remarkable Resurrection Church, overlooking the Debra River, on the right.

The overall unity of the city was lost in the 1930s with the destruction of its main focus – that is, the ensemble comprising the Trinity and Dormition cathedrals and their bell towers. This act of vandalism has been aggravated in recent decades by a mindless programme of construction along the Volga which has filled the very finest vistas with depressing blocks of flats. Fortunately, however, the classical quarter, together with its principal buildings, has remained largely unspoilt, as have the magnificent sixteenth- and seventeenth-century masterpieces on the edge of the city.

The history of Kostroma begins in the twelfth century, when the Slavs first colonized the Volga area. The city was probably founded by Yuri Dolgoruky in 1152, when he commenced construction of Pereslavl-Zalessky and other towns in his territory.

In the thirteenth century Kostroma became the capital of its own 'appanage' principality. It shared the fate of all of Suzdalian Rus during the Tatar ravages of 1237. The city was rebuilt during the long reign of Vasily Yaroslavich (1243-76), when the Cathedral of the Dormition was built and the Monastery of Our Saviour was restored. Kostroma slowly spread itself along the banks of the Sula River, which joins the Volga on its left, north bank a little below the River Kostroma. The main part of the city, together with the oldest monasteries, was on the Sula's right bank; the area on the left bank was known as Debra (meaning a dense or impassable forest), where the Church of the Resurrection was rebuilt in the thirteenth century. Today, the Sula is an underground river which plays no visible part in Kostroma's cityscape.

The Ipatiev Monastery, on the right bank of the Kostroma near its confluence with the Volga, was founded in 1332. According to legend, a Tatar chieftain, Tchet, was struck down by illness on this spot while on a political mission to the Grand Duke of Muscovy. Tchet had a vision of the Virgin with the Apostle Philip and St Ipatiev, who promised that he would be restored to health if he embraced Christianity. Once recovered, Tchet completed his journey to Muscovy, was converted to Christianity, and later founded a monastery dedicated to St Ipatiev at the spot where he had seen the vision. The Godunov family was descended from this same Tchet, and were patrons of the monastery for several centuries.

Kostroma became part of Muscovy in 1329, during the reign of Grand Duke Ivan Kalita (1328-40), whose nickname, 'Moneybags', derives from his role as tribute collector for the Tatars. Its remoteness from the main Russian principalities spared it from some of the worst

The Trinity Cathedral in the Ipatiev Monastery, domes and general view from the northwest. The main, north façade of the cathedral has a large blind arcade; the *shirinki* on the pilasters of its gallery and on the porch are continued right down to ground level.

Kostroma

spoilations of the Tatars in the fourteenth century. It was to the Ipatiev Monastery, with its stout oak fortifications, that the Muscovite Grand Duke Dmitri Donskoy and his family fled from the invading Tokhtamysh in 1382; and in 1408, Vasily Dmitrievich, Grand Duke of Muscovy, found refuge here from the forays of Khan Yedigea.

In the early fifteenth century Kostroma became a city of considerable importance, with thirty churches to its name. As in most of northern Russia, the majority of its buildings were of wood. The densely built streets were very vulnerable to fire, and two serious conflagrations, in 1413 and 1416, virtually destroyed the city; indeed, a chronicle of 1416 relates that 'Vasily Dmitrievich refounded the city of Kostroma'. In fact, the fortress was moved a short distance down-river along the Volga, where new earth ramparts, fortified with oak walls and fourteen towers, were constructed.

In Kostroma, as in many other Russian cities, the economic prosperity of the sixteenth century led to a period of intense building activity. The Dormition and Trinity cathedrals were rebuilt, and Kostroma's oldest surviving building, the cathedral of the fourteenth-century Epiphany Monastery, was erected between 1559 and 1565. This is a five-domed cuboid structure set on a high plinth with an arched gallery on three sides; the walls are decorated with fine pilasters and cornices; the drums beneath the domes are embellished with blind arcades.

The next phase in Kostroma's artistic development was associated with the rise of the Godunovs, during the reign of Tsar Fyodor Ioannovich (1584-98), when Boris Godunov's sister Irina became Tsaritsa. Wishing to emphasize the antiquity and prestige of their city, the Godunovs made lavish gifts to the Ipatiev Monastery which financed new buildings and works of art. Between 1585 and and 1590 the monastery's wooden fortifications were replaced by a stone wall nearly 20 feet high and a mile long, with towers at the corners, two towers at the gates, and two churches over the gates. The churches were dedicated to Saint Irina and Saint Fyodor, whose namesakes were the royal couple themselves – Irina and Fyodor Stratilat. The monastery's Trinity Cathedral, whose murals and exterior painting were commissioned by Boris Godunov, was also built at this time – it was completed in 1596.

The dreadful events of the Polish and Swedish invasions in the early 1600s impinged upon Kostroma; but some of the most heroic pages of its history were also written at this period. The city was seized by the Poles in 1608 but quickly liberated by resistance forces from Galich and Kostroma itself. Early in 1609 Kostroma again fell to the Poles, who were, however, forced to quit the city in March of that year and withdraw behind the walls of the Ipatiev Monastery. After a siege lasting six months the patriotic *opolcheniye* (national popular army) stormed the monastery and expelled the Poles – thanks mainly to the courage of two Kostromans, Konstantin Mezentsev and Nikolai Kostigin, who detonated a barrel of gunpowder in an underground passage beneath the monastery walls.

In 1612 many citizens of Krostoma joined the *opolcheniye* organized by two great patriots, Kuzma Minin and Prince Dmitri Pozharsky, to liberate Muscovy and all Russian territories. In 1613 the Assembly of the Land elected Mikhail Romanov as Tsar, then living in the Ipatiev Monastery. A delegation was sent to the monastery to inform Mikhail Romanov of the will of the nation. However, a Polish force, dispatched to capture the newly elected Tsar, reached Kostroma at the same time. Not far from the city, a peasant, Ivan Susanin, came across this enemy column wandering about, lost. Under the pretext of collaboration Susanin led them into dense forest where they were at the mercy of the local defenders, an act of heroic defiance for which he paid with his life. (His story is the basis for Glinka's opera *A Life for the Tsar*.) The Ipatiev Monastery subsequently became a sacred place for the Romanovs, who visited it frequently and supported it generously.

Kostroma emerged from the Time of Troubles so depopulated and impoverished that in 1614 it contained only 312 households. It recovered quickly, however, and by 1650 that number had risen to 2,080. Kostroma became the fourth most important economic centre of Russia; on the Volga it was second only to Yaroslavl. Smithery, soap manufacture, tanning and linen production all contributed to its burgeoning prosperity. In the second half of the seventeenth century Kostroman builders and artists became famous for their work in many cities in Russia and in the Imperial Armoury of the Kremlin.

Interior of the Trinity Cathedral in the Ipatiev Monastery. The frescoes date from 1685, and are the work of the outstanding *artel* led by Guri Nikitin and Sila Savin. They are divided into five rows: the top row depicts the appearance of angels to Abraham and to Lot; beneath it are two rows of New Testament scenes; the lower rows contain scenes from the lives of the Apostles and allegories derived from the Song of Songs, and an ornamental panel.

Two views of the iconostasis of the Trinity Cathedral in the Ipatiev Monastery (1758), the work of the Kostroma carvers Zolotarev and Bykov. The five tiers are decorated with volutes and ninety-two columns, each one finely worked from a single piece of wood. The carving of the Royal Doors is particularly elaborate. Several sixteenth-century icons were transferred to the iconostasis from the old cathedral, but the majority belong to the seventeenth and eighteenth centuries.

Kostroma

Rooms built over the cellars of the Ipatiev Monastery between the sixteenth and early eighteenth centuries.

Kostroma

The Palace of the Romanov Boyars in the Ipatiev Monastery. The first buildings on this site were erected between 1586 and 1588. From 1598 they served as the residence of the Father Superior. In 1613 two second-floor rooms on the south side were occupied by Mikhail Romanov. In the mid-eighteenth century, the extremely dilapidated building underwent an extensive, rather romantic, restoration supervised by the academic architect Fyodor Rikhter. A grand royal staircase was built, the interior was redecorated, and the exterior was painted to give a faceted effect.

The centre of the city still consisted of the fifteenth-century fortress-citadel, the Dormition and Trinity cathedrals, the residence of the military governor and the houses of rich boyars and lesser nobility. In 1619, however, the citadel became the 'Old Citadel' (*Stary Gorod*), when a 'New Citadel' (*Novy Gorod*), was built – like the earlier one – in wood, on its northern rim. The new area included a market, customs post, weigh-house and two wooden churches, all enclosed by a wall with twelve towers.

Kostroma's fortifications were reinforced between 1642 and 1648 by the addition of stone walls and six towers to the Epiphany Monastery. These were dismantled in the nineteenth century; all that remains today is one octagonal tower which was later rebuilt as a tent-roofed bell tower. The Ipatiev Monastery walls were reinforced, and those of the Novy Gorod rebuilt.

In 1649, while the new city wall was under construction, the city's Trinity Cathedral was destroyed when gunpower stored in its lower floor exploded by accident. The cathedral was quickly rebuilt, being completed in 1652. Its composition largely repeats that of the sixteenth-century building – a basic cuboid structure on a high plinth with a two-storey gallery around it and five domes; but there is much new detail. For example, the traditional appearance of the *zakomary* was altered by the insertion of small imposts (horizontal blocks) above the pilasters leading up to them; the galleries were enclosed; the cathedral's main, north façade, facing the inner court, was decorated with a large blind arcade; the small columns and parapets were decorated with rows of recessed panels, called *shirinki*, which on the north façade descended to the lower storey; and, finally, a large tent-roofed porch, with pendant shapes – *girki* – was built onto the north side. The parents of Boris Godunov lie buried in the cathedral.

In 1652 the cathedral's three portals were fitted with splendid sixteenth-century bronze and gold doors donated by Dmitri Godunov. Scenes from the Old and New Testaments, together with the Evangelists and Prophets are depicted on them in gold on black.

The Trinity Cathedral's frescoes were begun in 1653, but a serious fire in 1654, followed by a plague (whose victims included Vasily Ilyn Zapokrovsky, a leading artist of the team at work on the mural), halted progress. Work was later resumed and completed in 1685 by the distinguished *artel* led by Guri Nikitin and Sila Savin, who were also permanently engaged in the decoration of the royal court and many churches in Yaroslavl, Rostov and Pereslavl-Zalessky.

A great carved throne, presented by Mikhail Fyodorovich Romanov, was placed in the cathedral (it is now in the Kolomenskoye Museum in Moscow). The cathedral's outstanding iconostasis, carved and with gilding on a black background, dates from 1756-58 but includes sixteenth- and seventeenth-century icons.

Woodcarving was a prominent feature of seventeenth-century art, and the art collection of the Kostroma Museum of History and Architecture in the Ipatiev Monastery contains splendid examples of carved wooden icons and painted wooden statuary dating from this period, as well as an interesting selection of painted icons and applied art.

The bell tower to the west of the Ipatiev Trinity Cathedral was begun in 1601. The oldest section (1601-04) stands 98 feet high and has a three-tiered belfry, which contained nineteen bells. Originally, all three of these tiers were open and the tower had three hipped roofs. In 1649 a striking clock was placed in the south flight of the middle tier and a four-tiered tent-roofed tower with green tiles was added.

The monastery's archiepiscopal quarters were situated in the northwest corner. The lower floor dates from the sixteenth century; the upper floors were added in the seventeenth and eighteenth centuries. The east wall was abutted by a row of monks' cells, over which the Church of Saints Chrisanth and Darya, designed by the architect Konstantin Ton (1794-1881), was built between 1841 and 1863. The north and west walls, with access via the Catherine Gate (eighteenth century), enclosed several sixteenth- to eighteenth-century buildings, including the residence of the Romanov boyars, restored in 1863.

The settlement around the Ipatiev Monastery, separated from the city by the Kostroma River, sharply increased in size after the construction of a reservoir on the Volga (which respected and preserved the original appearance of the countryside). This was to prove a perfect setting for the open-air Museum of Wooden Architecture (one of the earliest in Russia), which was inaugurated here in 1955.

Kostroma

Left

The Church of Our Saviour from the village of Spass-Bezhy (1628). Originally situated on low-lying land which was prone to flooding, the church was built on tall oak piles. Access was from the south; a bell tower formerly stood on its west side. The church was transferred to the grounds of the Ipatiev Monastery in the 1950s.

Right

The Church of the Cathedral of the Mother of God, from the village of Kholm (1552), now in the Kostroma Museum of Wooden Architecture. View from the west. Originally, the church would have been built with a tent roof; the present five-domed array on intersecting *bochki* (gables) probably dates from the eighteenth century.

Kostroma

The Novy Gorod enclosure now displays a collection of wooden bath-houses and the Church of the Transfiguration of Our Saviour, from the nearby village of Spass-Bezhy. These exhibits, all originally from areas liable to spring floods, are still raised high above the ground on their wooden piles. The church is especially noteworthy: it is small, but its overhanging galleries and steeply sloping roofs combine to create a truly majestic effect, while the stilts lifting it above the ground give it the appearance of a fantastical vision which appears to float in the air.

The main part of the open-air museum is situated north of the Ipatiev Monastery and the Church of St John the Divine. In recent decades many wooden houses, mills, bath-houses and several churches have been transferred to the site. In spite of the artificiality of the museum situation, these objects have created an original and convincing environment of their own – a charming extension to the landscape of Kostroma which to some extent makes up for the destruction of the main cathedral ensemble in the 1930s. The museum's oldest church is the Cathedral of the Virgin from the village of Kholm, near Galich, dating from 1552. The large main octagon bears another, shorter and narrower; four decorative gables, placed in the form of a cross, are crowned by five domes. The little *trapeznaya* is surrounded by very broad overhanging galleries adjoining the main building, reached via a porch on the west façade. The rhythmical effect created by the gently sloping roofs is particularly expressive. The *trapeznaya*, whose exterior seems very wide, is small and narrow inside, compared with the large main octagonal structure.

Possibly the finest building on the east side of Kostroma is the Church of the Resurrection on the Debra (1652), which was paid for by a rich merchant, Kiril Isakov, and other traders of Kostroma. It is important not only for its size but for the complexity and richness of its design. The main building, surrounded by a gallery, has five domes. There are three porches with high tent roofs, and a chapel dedicated to the Three Kings situated at the northeast corner. These roofs mingle with the three hipped roofs and the domes of the Holy Gate in front of the west façade to create an interesting silhouette. Originally the ensemble included a tent-roofed bell tower (dismantled in 1801).

The church's Holy Gates consist of two arches, the larger leading to the church and the smaller to the inner courtyard. Short, broad pillars serve to support both arches; high up on the walls the *shirinki* display carvings of animals and birds; a lion and an eagle, a unicorn symbolizing chastity, and an *alkonost* – a bird with a crowned human head, symbolizing the souls of the righteous.

The church was painted immediately after building was completed, and some original fragments of this painting were discovered in the gallery (which includes some beautiful portals) and on the drums of the domes during restoration work in the 1870s. The mural in the Chapel of the Three Kings dates from the 1670s, and is of very high quality and in an excellent state of preservation. The carved altar iconostasis, a masterpiece of decorative art, is entirely covered with delicate carved and gilded ornamentation. The Royal Doors are framed by a deep arch – in effect a portal – with pairs of slender columns at the sides.

Life in Kostroma, as in all the Volga cities, slowed down considerably after the Russian capital was transferred from Moscow to St Petersburg in the eighteenth century. However, Kostroma's medieval streets and architecture remained largely intact until 1773, when fire destroyed the Old and New citadels, together with a large part of the market quarter. An urban development plan, carried out between 1775 and 1781, imposed radical change on the layout of the medieval quarters and streets. The Stary Gorod retained its historical and religious significance, but the main focus for new development was now to be the Novy Gorod, where a square, with streets leading from it in a fan-shaped pattern, was created. This classical plan, comprising the square, streets and spacious market, gave the city a fresh, new aspect which still retains its charm.

The Church of Our Saviour from the village of Fominskoye (1712), now in the Kostroma Museum of Wooden Architecture. A small church of log construction, adjoined on the west side by a large refectory with a fine octagonal bell tower above it, and an ornamented porch; a particularly attractive effect is created by the different shapes of the roofs on the porch, the refectory and the church itself.

Kostroma